THE "QUOTABLE" LINCOLN

A Selection from the Writings and
Speeches of Abraham Lincoln

compiled and edited by
EDWARD STEERS, JR.

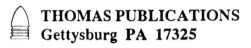

THOMAS PUBLICATIONS
Gettysburg PA 17325

Cover design by Ryan C. Stouch

TABLE OF CONTENTS

A. Lincoln.
(U.S. Army Mil. Hist. Inst.)

PREFACE

More than one hundred and thirty years have now passed since Abraham Lincoln carefully placed his last thoughts on paper. Carefully is perhaps more appropriate to Abraham Lincoln than to most other figures in history, presidential or literary. To the very end of his life, Lincoln was a student of the English language and its use as a means of communication. He continually studied his native language and devoted considerable energies to everything he wrote. He often evaluated and criticized his own writings even after he had officially finished with them. An example of this can be found in his Gettysburg Address. Popular myth had Lincoln jot down the few lines of his immortal address while riding the train to Gettysburg. Nothing could have been further from the truth. Lincoln worked and reworked his "few appropriate remarks" with painstaking thoughtfulness. Even after the final draft was delivered Lincoln had his doubts as to its effectiveness. The principal speaker at Gettysburg was the famous statesman orator, Edward Everett, who wrote Lincoln following the dedication ceremonies congratulating him on his memorable words. Lincoln showed his concern when he wrote Everett back,

> *I am pleased to know that, in your judgement, the little I did say was not entirely a failure.*

Lincoln knew the power of the written word and was attracted to those writers who excelled in its form. He was so enamored of William Shakespeare that he had committed certain of his plays to memory and could recite them at the drop of a hat. Macbeth was his favorite.

During the one hundred and thirty plus years since Lincoln's death, numerous books and collected works have appeared centering on his writings and speeches. These works have ranged in format from encyclopedias listing quotations by subject in alphabetical form to attempts to gather chronologically every scrap of writing and documented speech or utterance attributed to Lincoln. Included among these efforts are several booklets or pamphlets which collect the "momentous" or "historically significant" writings of Lincoln.

But Lincoln's great qualities are so much more than that reflected in his "greatest writings." Only when one looks across the breadth of his literary work does one begin to appreciate the real greatness of this extraordinary person. Lincoln's quality of humanness and compassion, his keen insight into human nature, his uncanny ability to see to the heart of a problem and his ability to persuade his strongest critics to understand, if not accept, the wisdom of his views, is seen again and again in his writings whether scribbling a note to pardon a condemned soldier or explaining his position on the emancipation of slaves.

It is the intention and scope of this book to present a sampling of Lincoln's writing over a wide range of subjects, trivial as well as momentous. It is the author's opinion that the qualities which endear most of the world to Lincoln are to be found in a multitude of places not limited to the Gettysburg Address or his inaugural speeches, but also found in his writing about socks or trouble with his generals, or his little boy Tad.

The selections are not arranged chronologically because Lincoln's skills as a writer show little evolution chronologically and would add little to the theme of this work. I have included the first known writing as well as the last only for those who insist on a beginning and an end to such things.

It is hard for me to imagine that anyone who reads across the length of Abraham Lincoln's writings will not be entranced with the beauty of his expression and the superiority of his intellect, whether already an admirer or a critic.

In the bibliography listed at the end of this book, several works are listed which the reader will find interesting should he or she wish to pursue the subject further. While some are long out of print, they are still available through used book stores. Happy reading.

THE "QUOTABLE" LINCOLN

A Selection from the Writings and
Speeches of Abraham Lincoln

THE IMAGERY OF LINCOLN

To many, the most notable characteristic of Abraham Lincoln lay in his special ability to express himself in ways that were not only easy for his listener to grasp, but which conveyed his meaning in illustrative imagery.

Lincoln's command of the English language was unique in many ways. While both his written and spoken thoughts seemed effortless in most instances, Lincoln was a careful student and therefore skillful master at communication. He respected the meaning of words and spoke with a clarity that could be understood by all alike. He was not an extensive reader, but was a keen observer of everything around him. What he did read he tended to learn fully and, according to his law partner William Herndon, he had a photographic memory for anything that caught his interest.

Lincoln's use of imagery stemmed in part from his early "prairie years." His pioneer heritage was replete with symbolism and images which served him throughout his adult life. Time and again he would use examples taken from the prairies of Illinois and the wooded frontier of Indiana. Lincoln's use of imagery was also founded in his considerable knowledge of the Bible and Acsop's Fables as well as his mastery of much of William Shakespeare. These works formed the foundation for much of Lincoln's style as a writer and speaker. As Lincoln himself explained, his storytelling and humorous anecdotes were not so much to amuse as they were to effectively convey a point. And points thus made are almost always points well taken. Lincoln knew this and was a master at its effectiveness. He could state profound thoughts simply.

Lincoln was naturally figurative in his style and it added greatly to the richness of his writings. He had an ear for rhythm which often resulted in a poetic style to his writing. Consider the rhythm and imagery Lincoln used in his closing remarks of his first inaugural speech in which he appeals to the southern secessionists to hold to the Union:

I am loath to close. We are not enemies, but friends. We must not be enemies. Though passion may have strained, it must not break our bonds of affection. The mystic chords of memory, stretching from every battle-field, and patriot grave, to every living heart and hearthstone, all over this broad land, will yet swell the chorus of the Union, when again touched, as surely they will be, by the better angels of our nature.

Consider the imagery in the following phrases found in the Gettysburg Address: *...our fathers brought forth, ...conceived in liberty, ...the last full measure of devotion, ...a new birth of freedom.*

And in his second inaugural speech Lincoln again uses imagery to effect his point: *...until every drop of blood drawn with the lash, shall be paid by another drawn with the sword;* and still further, *...to bind up the nation's wounds.*

In his message to Congress early in his second term Lincoln cautioned his colleagues with the following words: *The fiery trial through which we pass, will light us down, in honor or dishonor, to the latest generation.* Or when justifying black suffrage on the grounds that those admitted to the polls would help *...keep the jewel of liberty within the family of freedom.*

These phrases are reminiscent of Shakespeare in their imagery. They possess a poetic quality and rhythm that is almost sing-song in style.

Lincoln, however, was also capable of imagery which was considerably more common in its appeal. In referring to Salmon P. Chase, his Secretary of the Treasury, Lincoln said that Chase *had a presidential chin-fly biting him.* Referring to arguments on slavery, Lincoln said: *The argument has got down as thin as soup made by boiling the shadow of a pigeon that has starved to death.*

Lincoln's generals were a favorite target of his metaphors. In referring to McClellan's repeated complaints that he never had enough troops, he commented: *Sending men to that army of the Potomac is like shoveling fleas across a barnyard — not half of them get there.* In referring to Meade's failure to follow up his victory at Gettysburg by allowing Lee's army to escape over the Potomac, Lincoln wrote: *We had gone through all the labor of tilling and planting an enormous crop, and when it was ripe we did not harvest it.*

To his favorite general, Ulysses S. Grant, Lincoln wrote: *Hold on with a bulldog grip, and chew and choke as much as possible.* And to Joseph Hooker as Lee was making his way into Pennsylvania:

> *If the head of Lee's army is at Martinsburg* (West Virginia) *and the tail of it on the Plank road between Fredericksburg and Chancellorsville, the animal must be very slim somewhere: could you not break him?*

In referring to his Navy, Lincoln dubbed it *Uncle Sam's Webfeet,* and to the coast of the United States as, *the watery margins.* When Vicksburg and Port Hudson fell in July of 1863 Lincoln commented, *The Father of Waters again goes unvexed to the sea.*

It was Lincoln's habit to set aside a block of time every morning to allow the people to come see him and tell him what was on their mind. Lincoln referred to these sessions as his *public opinion baths.* He also referred to them as his *promiscuous receptions,* where *every applicant for audience has to take his turn as if waiting to be shaved in a barber shop.* The constant badgering from office seekers who lined up every morning occasioned the comment that: *There are too many pigs for the tits.*

In responding to a neighbor's question as to what was upsetting Lincoln's two boys as Lincoln held them at arm's length while they tried to kick and punch each other he replied: *Why, just what's wrong with the whole world. I've got three walnuts and each wants two.*

In referring to one of Stephen Douglas' arguments during the great debates, Lincoln characterized Douglas' reasoning: *...by which a man can prove a horse-chestnut to be a chestnut horse.*

The greatness of Lincoln was not because of his mastery of expression or his uncanny ability to twist a phrase. To be sure, those qualities won him a great many admirers and convinced a certain number of skeptics. Lincoln's greatness lay in his vision of the nation and his steadfast principals to which that nation would adhere as it made its way toward the twentieth century. In his speeches and writings none need doubt exactly where Lincoln was taking all of us. His use of vivid metaphor and simile helped smooth out the road along which he asked us to travel.

IN THE BEGINNING...

The following verse represents the earliest known writing by Lincoln. It is found in surviving fragments of Lincoln's self-made arithmetic book which had been preserved by his step-mother Sarah Bush Johnston Lincoln. These fragments are dated to 1824 when Lincoln was fifteen years old.

Abraham Lincoln is my name
And with my pen I wrote the same
I wrote in both haste and speed
and left it here for fools to read

LINCOLN ON LINCOLN

I was born in Kentucky, raised in Indiana, reside in Illinois.

The following is his speech to the people of Sangamo County at the time of his candidacy for the state general assembly. Lincoln came in eighth in a field of thirteen but carried his own precinct, 277 votes out of 300 cast (92%). Lincoln lived in the village of New Salem, Illinois at the time of his candidacy.

March 9, 1832

Fellow-Citizens: ...I was born and have ever remained in the most humble walks of life. I have no wealthy or popular relations to recommend me. My case is thrown exclusively upon the independent voters of this county, and if elected they will have conferred a favor upon me, for which I shall be unremitting in my labors to compensate. But if the good people in their wisdom shall see fit to keep me in the background, I have been too familiar with disappointments to be very much chagrined... Your friend and fellow-citizen,

A. Lincoln

Abraham Lincoln in 1858.
(U.S. Army Mil. Hist. Inst.)

From a descriptive note to Jesse W. Fell:

J.W. Fell, Esq.   *Springfield,*
My dear Sir: *Dec. 20. 1859*

Herewith is a little sketch, as you requested. There is not much of it, for the reason, I suppose, that there is not much of me.

If any thing be made out of it, I wish it to be modest, and not to go beyond the material.

...My parents were both born in Virginia, of undistinguished families—second families, perhaps I should say...when I came of age I did not know much. Still somehow, I could read, write, and cipher to the Rule of Three; but that was

all.... The little advance I now have upon this store of infor-
mation, I have picked up from time to time under the pressure
of necessity.

If any personal description of me is thought desirable, it
may be said, I am, in height, six feet, four inches, nearly; lean
in flesh, weighing, on an average, one hundred and eighty
pounds; dark complexion, with coarse black hair, and grey
eyes—no other marks or brands recollected. Yours very truly

A. Lincoln

From a speech delivered to the 140th Illinois Volunteer Infantry, March 17, 1865:

I was born in Kentucky, raised in Indiana, reside in Illi-
nois.

When told that one of his neighbors had remarked: *"I can't*
understand those speeches of Lincoln," Lincoln responded, *There are*
always some fleas a dog can't reach.

Sandberg, *The Prairie Years.*

On August 23, 1864, Lincoln met with his cabinet and asked
each member to sign blind a slip of paper which he circulated
among them. At the time, Lincoln's chances for reelection in
the fall elections appeared unlikely to most politicos; not so
among the common electorate, however.

Executive mansion
Washington, August 23, 1864.

This morning, as for some days past, it seems exceedingly
probable that this administration will not be re-elected. Then
it will be my duty to so co-operate with the President elect, as
to save the Union between the election and the inauguration;
as he will have secured his election on such ground that he
can not possibly save it afterwards.

A. Lincoln

During the great debates of 1858, Stephen A. Douglas referred to Lincoln as "two faced" to which Lincoln replied:

I leave it to my audience. If I had another face, do you think I'd wear this one?

Reported by Major General Egbert L. Viele in a conversation with Lincoln in which Lincoln told Viele:

If I have one vice, it is not to be able to say no! Thank God, for not making me a woman, but if He had, I suppose He would have made me just as ugly as He did, and no one would ever have tempted me.

"CONNECTIONS"
LINCOLN'S TERM FOR RELATIONS

You are not lazy, and still you are an idler.

To His Father, Thomas Lincoln:

My dear Father: *Washington, Decr. 24th. 1848.*

Your letter of the 7th. was received night before last. I very cheerfully send you the twenty dollars, which sum you say is necessary to save your land from sale. It is singular that you should have forgotten a judgement against you; and it is singular that the plaintiff should have let you forget it so long, particularly as I suppose you have always had property enough to satisfy a judgement of that amount. Before you pay it, it would be well to be sure you have not paid it; or, at least, that you can not prove you have paid. Give my love to Mother, and all the connections. Affectionately your Son

A. Lincoln

To his stepbrother, John D. Johnston. Continuing as a part of the same letter to his father, Lincoln answers his stepbrother John D. Johnston's request for yet another loan:

Dear Johnston:

Your request for eighty dollars, I do not think it best, to comply with now. At the various times when I helped you a little, you have said to me "We can get along very well now" but in a very short time I find you in the same difficulty again. Now this can only happen by some defect in your conduct. What that defect is, I think I know. You are not lazy, and still you are an idler. I doubt whether since I saw you, you have done a good whole day's work, in any one day. You do not very much dislike to work; and still you do not work much, merely because it does not seem to you that you could get much for it. This habit of uselessly wasting time, is the whole difficulty; and it is vastly important to you, and still more so to your children that you should break this habit. It is more important to them, because they have longer to live, and can keep out of an idle habit before they are in it; easier than they can get out after they are in.

You are now in need of some ready money; and what I propose is, that you shall go to work, "tooth and nails" for some body who will give you money for it. Let Father and the boys take charge of things at home—prepare for a crop, and make the crop; and you go to work for the best money wages, or in discharge of any debt that you owe, that you can get. And to secure you a fair reward for your labor, I now promise you, that for every dollar you will, between this and the first of next May, get for your own labor, either in money, or in your own indebtedness, I will then give you one other dollar. By this, if you hire yourself at ten dollars a month, from me you will get ten more, making twenty dollars a month for your work. In this, I do not mean you shall go off to St. Louis, or the lead mines, or the gold mines, in Calif, but I mean for you to go at it for the best wages you can get close to home in Coles county. Now if you will do this, you will soon be out of debt, and what is better, you will have a habit that will keep you from getting in debt again. But if I should now clear you *out, next year you will be just as deep in as ever. You say you would almost give your place in Heaven for $70 or $80. Then you value your place in Heaven very cheaply for I am sure you can with the offer I make you get the seventy or eighty dollars for four or five months work. You say if I furnish you the money you will deed me the land, and, if you don't pay the money back, you will deliver possession. Nonsense! If you can't now live with the land, how will you then live without it? You have always been kind to me, and I do not now mean to be unkind to you. On the contrary, if you will but follow my advice, you will find it worth more than eight times eighty dollars to you. Affectionately Your brother*

A. Lincoln

Lincoln writes again to his stepbrother, John D. Johnston, in response to learning that his father is dying. The letter is revealing in that it suggests a distance between Lincoln and his father which did not exist between Lincoln and his stepmother:

Dear Brother: *Springfield, Jany. 12. 1851-*

On the day before yesterday I received a letter from Harriett (Lincoln's niece, Harriet Chapman Hanks), *written at Greenup. She says she has just returned from your house; and that Father is very low, and will hardly recover. She also says you have written me two letters; and that although you do not expect me to come now, you wonder that I do not write. I received both your letters, and although I have not answered them, it is not because I have forgotten them, or been uninterested about them—but because it appeared to me I could write nothing which could do any good. You already know I desire that neither Father or Mother shall be in want of any comfort either in health or sickness while they live; and I feel sure you have not failed to use my name, if necessary, to procure a doctor, or any thing else for Father in his present sickness. My business is such that I could hardly leave home now, if it were not, as it is, that my own wife is sick-abed. (It is a case of baby-sickness, and I suppose is not dangerous.) I sincerely hope Father may yet recover his health; but at all*

Thomas Lincoln. *(Lincoln Memorial University)*

Grave of Thomas Lincoln and Sarah Bush Johnston Lincoln.
Shiloh Baptist Church Cemetery near Charleston, Illinois.
(Photograph by author)

events tell him to remember to call upon, and confide in, our great, and good, and merciful Maker; who will not turn away from him in any extremity. He notes the fall of a sparrow, and numbers the hairs of our heads; and He will not forget the dying man, who puts his trust in Him. Say to him that if we could meet now, it is doubtful whether it would not be more painful than pleasant; but that if it be his lot to go now, he will soon have a joyous meeting with many loved ones gone before; and where the rest of us, through the help of God, hope ere-long to join them.

Write me again when you receive this.

A. Lincoln

Thomas Lincoln died three days later on January 15, 1851. He is buried with his second wife, Sarah Bush Johnston Lincoln in the Shiloh Baptist Church cemetery near Charleston, Illinois.

❖ ❖ ❖

Elizabeth Todd Grimsley was the daughter of Dr. John Todd, Mary Lincoln's uncle. Cousin Lizzie was one of Mary Lincoln's favorite cousins. She attended Lincoln's Inaugural Ball in 1861 and stayed on at the White House for six months visiting with Abraham and Mary. Like most of the family, she tried to gain from Lincoln's election by requesting a postmistress job for herself and a Naval Academy appointment for her son.

John T. Stuart, Lincoln's old law partner in Springfield and former mentor received a letter from Lincoln concerning Cousin Lizzie's request:

Private

Dear Stuart: *Washington, March 30, 1861*

Cousin Lizzie shows me your letter of the 27th. The question of giving her the Springfield Post-office troubles me. You see I have already appointed William Jayne a territorial Governor, and Judge Trumbull's brother to a Land-office. Will it do for me to go on and justify the declaration that Trumbull and I have divided out all the offices among our relatives? Dr. Wallace (Dr. William Wallace who married Fanny Todd, Mary Lincoln's sister), *you know, is needy, and looks to me; and I personally owe him much.*

I see by the papers, a vote is to be taken as to the Post-office. Could you not set up Lizzie and beat them all? She, being here, need know nothing of it, & therefore there would be no indelicacy on her part. Yours as ever,

A. Lincoln

Lizzie didn't get the job. She did, however, gain her son an appointment to the Naval Academy:

Mrs. Elizabeth J. Grimsley   *Washington, D.C.*
Springfield, Illinois   *June 6. 1863.*

Is your John ready to enter Naval-School? If he is, telegraph me his full name.

A. Lincoln

Executive Mansion,   *Washington, August 14, 1863*

My dear Cousin Lizzie I have, by the law, two classes of appointments to make to the Naval-School—ten of each, to the year. The first class, according to law, must be of families of the meritorious Naval-Officers; while the other class does not have such restriction. You see at once that if I have a vacancy in the first class, I cannot appoint Johnny (John T. Grimsley) *to it; and I have intended for months, and still intend, to appoint him to the very first vacancy I can get in the other class. Yours very truly*

A. Lincoln

Mrs. Elizabeth J. Grimsley   *Washington, D.C.*
Springfield, Illinois   *August 24, 1863.*

I mail the papers to you today appointing Johnny to the naval School.

A. Lincoln

Elizabeth "Lizzie" Grimsley.
First cousin to Mary Lincoln.
(Illinois State Historical Library)

Dr. William Wallace.
Mary Lincoln's brother-
in-law and a close family
friend.   The Lincolns
named their third son,
William Wallace Lincoln,
after Dr. Wallace.
(Author's collection)

❖ ❖ ❖

Tad Lincoln, the Lincoln's youngest child:

The doll Jack is pardoned by order of the President.

A. Lincoln

Hon. Sec. of War.
    Tad wants some flags. Can he be accommodated?
April 10, 1865   *A. Lincoln*

April 10, 1865
    Let Master Tad have a Navy sword.

A. Lincoln

Will Mr. Dickson, Chief Engineer of Hibernia please pump the water out of a certain well, which Tad will show?
Feb.27,1865

A. Lincoln

My dear Sir   *Executive mansion, April 2. 1862.*

Allow me to thank you on behalf of my little son for your present of White rabbits. He is very much pleased with them.
Yours truly

Abraham Lincoln

Michael Crock Esq
860 N Fourth St. Philada.

From a check (five dollars) which Lincoln made out to his youngest son Tad who was recovering from an illness (believed to be typhoid fever) which took the life of his older brother Willie:

March 10, 1862

Pay to: "Tad" (when he is well enough to present)

A. Lincoln

❖   ❖   ❖

Lincoln writes to Mary in New York informing her of the death of her brother-in-law, Confederate Brigadier General Ben Hardin Helm. Helm is married to Mary's youngest sister Emily Todd Helm. Both Emily and Mary are devastated by the loss. Mary brings Emily to the White House to comfort her, giving rise to gossip that the President's wife is a Confederate sympathizer and agent.

Mrs. A. Lincoln   *Washington, D.C.*
Fifth Avenue Hotel, New York   *Sep. 24, 1863.*

We now have a tolerably accurate summing up of the late battle between Rosecrans and Bragg. The result is that we are worsted, if at all, only in the fact that we, after the main fighting was over, yielded the ground, thus leaving considerable of our artillery and wounded to fall into the enemies' hands, for which we got nothing in turn. We lost, in general officers, one killed, and three or four wounded, all Brigadiers; while according to rebel accounts, which we have, they lost six killed, and eight wounded. Of the killed, one Major Genl., and five Brigadiers, including your brother-in-law, Helm (Confederate Brigadier General Ben Hardin Helm—see Emily Helm correspondence); and of the wounded, three Major Generals, and five Brigadiers. This list may be reduced two in number, by correction of confusion in names. At 11/40 A.M. yesterday Gen. Rosecrans telegraphed from Chattanooga "We hold this point, and I can not be dislodged, except by very superior numbers, and after a great battle." A despatch leaving there after night yesterday says, "No fight to-day."

A. Lincoln

Mrs. Lincoln   *Executive mansion*
Philadelphia, Pa.   *Washington, June 9. 1863.*

Think you had better put "Tad's" pistol away. I had an ugly dream about him.

A. Lincoln

Mrs. Lincoln   *Executive mansion*
Philadelphia   *Washington 1863.*

*Your three despatches received. I am very well; and am
glad to know that you & "Tad" are so.*

A. Lincoln

❖ ❖ ❖

The Presidential Nanny Goat:

Executive Mansion,   *Washington, August 8, 1863.*

*My dear Wife. All is well as usual, and no particular
trouble anyway. I put the money into the Treasury at five per
cent, with the privlege* (sic) *of withdrawing it any time upon
thirty days' notice. I suppose you are glad to learn this. Tell
dear Tad, poor "Nanny Goat" is lost; and Mrs. Cuthbert & I
are in distress about it. The day you left Nanny was found
resting herself, and chewing her little cud, on the middle of
Tad's bed. But now she's gone! The gardener kept com-
plaining that she destroyed the flowers, till it was concluded
to bring her down to the White House. This was done, and
the second day she had disappeared, and has not been heard
of since. This is the last we know of poor "Nanny"*
    Affectionately

A. Lincoln

The Interesting Case of Emily T. Helm

What makes this particular case so interesting is the T. in
Emily T. Helm. It stands for Todd, the same Todd of Mary
Todd Lincoln. Emily Helm is the younger half sister of Mary
Todd Lincoln and one of Mary's favorites. She married Ben
Hardin Helm of Kentucky who became a Brigadier General in
the Confederate Army. While Mary Lincoln's brother-in-law
was a Confederate General officer, it was not unusual. Mary
Lincoln's family was well-laced with Confederate officers. Three
of Mary's step-sisters were married to Confederate officers

Emily Todd Helm. Younger sister of Mary Todd Lincoln.
(William H. Townsend collection)

which occasioned considerable whisperings about Mary
Lincoln's allegiance to the Northern cause.

Lincoln provided the young widow with safe conduct
through the Union lines allowing her to return to Kentucky
from Alabama.

L.B.Todd   *Lexington, Ky*
Washington, D.C.   *October 15th. 1863*

    I send the following pass to your care. A. Lincoln

                                        Washington D.C.
                                           Oct 15th. 63

"To whom it may concern
    *Allow Mrs Robert S. Todd, widow, to go south and bring
her daughter, Mrs. Genl B. Hardin Helm, with her children,
North to Kentucky.*
                                           A. Lincoln"

In December, Mary Lincoln had her half-sister come and stay in the White House for a period of six months during which the two women comforted each other in their bereavements, Emily having lost her husband and Mary, her young son Willie.

December 14, 1863
District of Columbia
Washington County

I, Emily T. Helm, do solemnly swear in presence of Almighty God that I will henceforth faithfully support, protect and defend the Constitution of the United States, and the union of the States thereunder; and that I will, in like manner, abide by, and faithfully support all acts of Congress passed during the existing rebellion with reference to slaves, so long and so far as not repealed, modified, or held void by Congress, or by decision of the Supreme Court; and that I will, in like manner, abide by, and faithfully support all like proclamations of the President, made during the existing rebellion, having reference to slaves so long and so far as not modified, or declared void by the Supreme Court. So help me God.

Executive Mansion,   *Washington, December 14, 1863.*

Mrs. Emily T. Helm, not being excepted from the benefits of the proclamation by the President of the United States issued on the 8th. day of December. 1863, and having on this day taken and subscribed the oath according to said proclamation, she is fully relieved of all penalties and forfeitures, and remitted to all her rights, all according to said proclamation, and not otherwise; and in regard to said restored rights of person and property, she is to be protected and afforded facilities as a loyal person.

Abraham Lincoln

P.S. Mrs. Helm claims to own some cotton at Jackson, Mississippi and also some in Georgia; and I shall be glad, upon either place being brought within our lines, for her to be afforded the proper facilities to show her ownership, and take her property.

Lincoln, somewhat apprehensive at having a Confederate general's wife in the White House, penned the following amnesty oath and letter for her safe conduct back to Kentucky after her stay. Although she used the letter more than once, there is no evidence that she ever signed the oath.

Executive Mansion
Washington, December 14, 1863.

Whom it may concern
    It is my wish that Mrs. Emily T. Helm, (widow of the late Gen. B. H. Helm, who fell in the Confederate service) now returning to Kentucky, may have protection of person and property, except as to slaves, of which I say nothing.

A. Lincoln

Office U.S. Military Telegraph,
War Department
Major General Burbridge
Lexington, Ky.
Washington, D.C., August 8th. 1864.

Last December Mrs. Emily T. Helm, half-sister of Mrs. L. and widow of the rebel general Ben. Hardin Helm stopped here on her way from Georgia to Kentucky, and I gave her a paper, as I remember, to protect her against the mere fact of her being Gen. Helm's widow. I hear a rumor to day that you recently sought to arrest her, but was prevented by her presenting the paper from me. I do not pretend to protect her against the consequences of disloyal words or acts, spoken or done by her since her return to Kentucky, and if the paper given her by me can be construed to give her protection for such words or acts, it is hereby revoked pro tanto. Deal with her for current conduct, just as you would with any other.

Despite all of Lincoln's gracious help to his wife's sister, Emily Helm remained embittered and vengeful toward Lincoln, writing him in 1864 that, "... your minie bullets have made us what we are."

COMPASSION

In this sad world of ours, sorrow comes to all;
and, to the young, it comes with bitterest agony,
because it takes them unawares.

At no other time does Lincoln show his keen sensitivity and humanness as he does in expressing his compassion to others in their time of grief. He had lost his mother when he was nine years old, his only sister when he was twenty, his son Eddie in 1850 and his son Willie within a year of occupying the White House. Lincoln, feeling the weight of grief many times in his life, had come to understand it better than most.

To Fanny McCullough: The daughter of Lieutenant Colonel William McCullough, 4th Illinois Cavalry, who was killed in a skirmish in Kansas on December 5, 1862. Lincoln was well acquainted with McCullough from his Illinois days.

Executive Mansion,
Washington, December 23, 1862.

Dear Fanny
    It is with deep grief that I learn of the death of your kind and brave Father; and especially, that it is affecting your young heart beyond what is common in such cases. In this sad world of ours, sorrow comes to all; and, to the young, it comes with bitterest agony, because it takes them unawares. The older have learned to ever expect it. I am anxious to afford some alleviation of your present distress. Perfect relief is not possible, except with time. You can not now realize that you will ever feel better. Is not this so? And yet it is a mistake. You are sure to be happy again. To know this, which is certainly true, will make you some less miserable now. I have had experience enough to know what I say; and you need only to believe it, to feel better at once. The memory of your dear Father, instead of an agony, will yet be a sad sweet feeling in your heart, of a purer, and holier sort than you have known before.

Please present my kind regards to your afflicted mother.
Your sincere friend

A. Lincoln

Fanny McCullough. **The young daughter of Lincoln's friend,**
Lieutenant Colonel William McCullough of the Fourth Illinois
cavalry. *(Illinois State Historical Society)*

Mrs. Bixby was a widow who lived in Boston, Massachusetts. Although Massachusetts Adjutant-General William Schouler was incorrect in informing Lincoln that five of Mrs. Bixby's sons had been killed in the war, Lincoln's letter assuming it to be true is one of his more poignant and beautiful letters.

Executive Mansion
Washington, Nov. 21, 1864.

Dear Madam,—I have been shown in the files of the War Department a statement of the Adjutant General of Massachusetts, that you are the mother of five sons who have died gloriously on the field of battle.

I feel how weak and fruitless must be any words of mine which should attempt to beguile you from any grief of a loss so overwhelming. But I cannot refrain from tendering to you the consolation that may be found in the thanks of the Republic they died to save.

I pray that our Heavenly Father may assuage the anguish of your bereavement, and leave you only the cherished memory of the loved and lost, and the solemn pride that must be yours, to have laid so costly a sacrifice upon the altar of Freedom. Yours, very sincerely and respectfully,

A. Lincoln

Postcard commemorating Lincoln's famous letter to the widow Lydia Bixby. (*Author's collection*)

Colonel Elmer Ellsworth (1837–1861). Ellsworth had read law in Lincoln's Springfield office in 1860 and his enthusiastic organizing skills impressed Lincoln greatly. He asked the young Ellsworth to accompany him on his inaugural trip to Washington. Immediately after war broke out, Ellsworth, with Lincoln's endorsement, was appointed Colonel of the 11th New York Volunteer Infantry—the famous Fire Zouaves. Ellsworth gained fame as a result of his untimely death while attempting to haul down the Confederate flag from a hotel located across the Potomac in Alexandria, Virginia on May 23, 1861. He was the first commissioned officer to die in the war and became the immediate martyr of the Northern cause. His assailant, James W. Jackson, proprietor of the hotel, served a similar role for the Southern cause.

Washington, D.C.
May 25. 1861

To the Father and Mother of Col.
Elmer E. Ellsworth:

My dear Sir and Madam, In the untimely loss of your noble son, our affliction here, is scarcely less than your own. So much of promised usefulness to one's country, and of bright hopes for one's self and friends, have rarely been so suddenly dashed, as in his fall. In size, and years, and in youthful appearance, a boy only, his power to command men, was surpassingly great. This power, combined with a fine intellect, an indomitable energy, and a taste altogether military, constituted in him, as seemed to me, the best natural talent, in that department, I ever knew. And yet he was singularly modest and deferential in social intercourse. My acquaintance with him began less than two years ago; yet through the latter half of the intervening period, it was as intimate as the disparity of our ages, and my engrossing engagements, would permit. To me, he appeared to have no indulgences or pastimes; and I never heard him utter a profane, or an intemperate word. What was conclusive of his good heart, he never forgot his parents. The honors he labored for so laudably, and, in the sad end, so gallantly gave his life, he meant for them, no less than for himself.

In the hope that it may be no intrusion upon the sacredness of your sorrow, I have ventured to address you this tribute to the memory of my young friend, and your brave and early fallen child.

May God give you that consolation which is beyond all earthly power. Sincerely your friend in a common conflict—

A. Lincoln

From a letter to Joshua Speed, February 25, 1842:

How miserably things seem to be arranged in this world. If we have no friends, we have no pleasure; and if we have them, we are sure to lose them, and be doubly pained by the loss.

To George C. Latham, A Springfield Neighbor:
The son of Philip C. Latham of Springfield, Illinois, George attended Phillips Exeter Academy with his neighbor and friend, Robert Todd Lincoln. Both boys applied to Harvard for admission. Robert was accepted, George was not.

My dear George   *Springfield, Ills. July 22, 1860.*

I have scarcely felt greater pain in my life than on learning yesterday from Bob's letter, that you had failed to enter Harvard University. And yet there is very little in it, if you will allow no feeling of discouragement to seize, and prey upon you. It is a certain truth, that you can enter, and graduate in, Harvard University; and having made the attempt, you must succeed in it. "Must" is the word.

I know not how to aid you, save in the assurance of one of mature age, and much severe experience, that you can not fail, if you resolutely determine, that you will not.

The President of the institution can scarcely be other than a kind man; and doubtless he would grant you an interview, and point out the readiest way to remove, or overcome, the obstacles which have thwarted you.

In your temporary failure there is no evidence that you may be a better scholar, and a more successful man in the great struggle of life, than many others, who have entered college more easily.

Again I say let no feeling of discouragement prey upon you, and in the end you are sure to succeed.

With more than a common interest I subscribe myself Very truly your friend,

A. Lincoln

Alas, George Latham did not get into Harvard. He enrolled in Yale only to leave after two years and return to Springfield, Illinois where he lived until his death in 1921.

The case of James Madison Cutts, Jr.:

> *Better give your path to a dog, than be bitten by him in contesting for the right.*

Captain James Madison Cutts, Jr., was the brother of Stephen A. Douglas' second wife, Adele A. Cutts. Cutts was tried before a court-martial board on June 30, 1863 on a charge of "conduct unbecoming an officer an a gentleman." Two of the specifications centered around Cutts having quarreled with a fellow officer and writing a derogatory letter concerning the officer. The third specification accused Cutts of secretively peering over a transom, while standing on a valise, into the room of a fellow officer while the officer's wife disrobed. The latter specification led Lincoln to remark to his private secretary, John Hay, that Cutts "should be elevated to the peerage with the title of Count Peeper."

Cutts pleaded "not guilty" to the first two specifications while acknowledging the third. The board found Cutts guilty on all three specifications and sentenced him to dismissal from the army. Lincoln, in light of Cutts' previous "gallant conduct in battle" remitted the sentence and instead issued Cutts an official reprimand which follows.

Executive mansion,
Capt. James M. Cutts   *Washington, Oct 26, 1863.*

> *Although what I am now to say is to be, in form, a reprimand, it is not intended to add a pang to what you have already suffered upon the subject to which it relates. You have too much of life yet before you, and have shown too much of promise as an officer, for your future to be lightly surrendered. You were convicted of two offences. One of them, not of great enormity, and yet greatly to be avoided, I feel you are in no danger of repeating. The other you are not so well assured against. The advice of a father to a son*

"Beware of entrance to a quarrel, but being in, bear it that the opposed may be aware of thee," is good, and yet not the best. Quarrel not at all. No man resolved to make the most of himself, can spare time for personal contention. Still less can he afford to take all the consequences, including the vitiating of his temper, and the loss of self-control. Yield larger things to which you can show no more than equal right; and yield lesser ones, though clearly your own. Better give your path to a dog, than be bitten by him in contesting for the right. Even killing the dog would not cure the bite.

In the mood indicated deal henceforth with your fellow men, and especially with your brother officers; and even the unpleasant events you are passing from will not have been profitless to you.

LINCOLN AND HIS GENERALS

What I now ask of you is military success,
and I will risk the dictatorship.

Lincoln, and the nation, suffered repeatedly in the early years of the war with a series of generals who seemed to lack the necessary aggressiveness to effectively pursue the various Confederate forces in the field. Not only did Lincoln suffer at the hands of professional commanders (West Pointers), but also with numerous "political" generals; those generals who held commissions in the voluntary forces and whose political credentials were essential to secure the support of certain critical constituencies throughout the North. Hence, War Democrats such as Nathaniel Preston Banks and Benjamin Franklin Butler, and Republicans such as Francis Preston Blair and James Shields were crucial to Lincoln's efforts and received coveted appointments to high command. Lincoln seemed to accept the predictable consequences of such "political" generalship until midway through the war when the cream began to rise to the top allowing him to appoint military leaders who were both aggressive and winners. Examples of Lincoln's correspondence to and about his problems with certain of his generals follows.

To Major General Joseph Hooker, recently appointed as head of the Army of the Potomac replacing Major General Ambrose E. Burnside. This represents Lincoln at his best.

Executive Mansion,
Washington, January 26, 1863

Major General Hooker:
General.

I have placed you at the head of the Army of the Potomac. Of course I have done this on what appear to me to be sufficient reasons. And yet I think it best for you to know that there are some things in regard to which, I am not quite satisfied with you. I believe you to be a brave and skillful soldier, which, of course, I like. I also believe you do not mix politics with your profession, in which you are right. You have confidence in yourself, which is a valuable, if not indispensable quality. You are ambitious, which, within reasonable bounds, does good rather than harm. But I think that during Gen. Burnside's command of the Army, you have taken counsel of your ambition, and thwarted him as much as you could, in which you did a great wrong to the country, and to a most meritorious and honorable brother officer. I have heard, in such a way as to believe it, of your recently saying that both the Army and the Government needed a Dictator. Of course, it was not for this, but in spite of it, that I have given you the command. Only those generals who gain successes, can set up dictators. What I now ask of you is military success, and I will risk the dictatorship. The government will support you to the utmost of its ability, which is neither more nor less than it has done or will do for all commanders. I much fear that the spirit which you have aided to infuse into the Army, of criticizing their Commander, and withholding confidence from him, will now turn upon you. I shall assist you as far as I can, to put it down. Neither you, nor Napoleon, if he were alive again, could get any good out of an army, while such a spirit prevailed in it.

And now, beware of rashness. Beware of rashness, but with energy, and sleepless vigilance, go forward, and give us victories.
Yours very truly

A. Lincoln

To Major General George B. McClellan, Commanding General, Army of the Potomac. An aggravated Lincoln writes McClellan approximately five weeks after the battle of Antietam clearly showing his frustration with McClellan who Lincoln characterized as *"having the slows."*

To Major General George B. McClellan Commanding
Washington City, D.C.
Oct. 24, 1862
Majr. Genl. McClellan
    I have just read your despatch about sore tongued and fatigued horses. Will you pardon me for asking what the horses of your army have done since the battle of Antietam that fatigue anything?

To Ambrose E. Burnside, recent commander of the Army of the Potomac now commander of the Army of the Ohio in the western theatre:

Office U.S. Military Telegraph,
War Department, Washington, D.C.,
Sep. 25. 1863.
Major General Burnside
    Yours of the 23rd. is just received, and it makes me doubt whether I am awake or dreaming. I have been struggling for ten days, first through Gen. Halleck, and then directly, to get you to go to assist Gen. Rosecrans in an extremity, and you have repeatedly declared you would do it, and yet you steadily move the contrary way. On the 19th. you telegraph once from Knoxville, and twice from Greenville, acknowledging receipt of order, and saying you will hurry support to Rosecrans. On the 20th. you telegraphed again from Knoxville, saying you will do all you can, and are hurrying troops to Rosecrans. On the 21st. you telegraph from Morristown,

saying you will hurry support to Rosecrans; and now your despatch of the 23rd. comes in from Carter's Station, still farther away from Rosecrans, still saying you will assist him, but giving no account of any progress made towards assisting him.

You came in upon the Tennessee River at Kingston, Loudon, and Knoxville; and what bridges or the want of them upon the Holston, can have to do in getting the troops towards Rosecrans at Chattanooga is incomprehensible. They (Burnside's troops) were already many miles nearer Chattanooga than any part of the Holston river is, and on the right side of it. If they are now on the wrong side of it, they can only have got so by going from the direction of Chattanooga, and that too, since you have assured us you would move to Chattanooga; while it would seem too, that they could recross the Holston, by whatever means they crossed it going East

A. Lincoln

And two days later:

Major General Burnside   *Washington, D.C.,*
Knoxville,Tenn.   *Sep. 27 1863*

Your despatch just received. My order to you meant simply that you should save Rosecrans from being crushed out, believing if he lost his position, you could not hold East Tennessee in any event; and that if he held his position, East Tennessee was substantially safe in any event. This despatch is in no sense an order. Gen. Halleck will answer you fully.

A. Lincoln

To Major General William S. Rosecrans in command of the Army of the Cumberland:

Executive mansion,
Washington, March 17, 1863.

Major General Rosecrans
...Now, as to your request that your Commission should date from December 1861. Of course you expected to gain

something by this; but you should remember that precisely so much as you would gain by it others would lose by it.

...I do not appreciate this matter of rank on paper, as you officers do. The world will not forget that you fought the battle of Stone River and it will never care a fig whether you rank Gen. Grant on paper, or he so, ranks you.

To Carl Schurz, a leader of the German-American community and a political general in his own right:

...I certainly have been dissatisfied with the slowness of Buell and McClellan; but before I relieved them I had great fears I should not find successors to them, who would do better; and I am sorry to add, that I have seen little since to relieve those fears.

Not all of Lincoln's correspondence with his generals resulted from frustration. The following letters, all to Ullyses S. Grant, reflect Lincoln's pleasure with his new general, who Lincoln characterized as a general *who fights.*

Following the surrender of Vicksburg on July 4, 1863, Lincoln courageously admits to Grant that, *...I was wrong.*

Major General Grant   *Executive Mansion,*
My dear General   *Washington, July 13, 1863.*

I do not remember that you and I ever met personally. I write this now as a grateful acknowledgement for the almost inestimable service you have done the country. I wish to say a word further. When you first reached the vicinity of Vicksburg, I thought you should do, what you finally did— march the troops across the neck, run the batteries with the transports, and thus go below; and I never had any faith, except a general hope that you knew better than I, that the Yazoo Pass expedition, and the like, could succeed. When you got below, and took Port-Gibson, Grand Gulf, and vicinity, I thought you should go down the river and join Gen. Banks; and when you turned Northward East of the Big Black, I feared it was a mistake. I now wish to make the personal acknowledgement that you were right, and I was wrong. Yours very truly,

A. Lincoln

Lieutenant General Ulysses S. Grant. *(Author's collection)*

Soon after appointing Grant Lieutenant General and General-in-Chief of all the Armies, Lincoln wrote:

> *Executive mansion,*
> *Washington, April 30, 1864.*
> *Lieutenant-General Grant,*
>   *Not expecting to see you again before the Spring campaign opens, I wish to express, in this way, my entire satisfaction with what you have done up to this time, so far as I*

understand it. The particulars of your plan I neither know, or seek to know. You are vigilant and self-reliant; and, pleased with this, I wish not to obtrude any constraints upon you. While I am very anxious that any great disaster, or the capture of our men in any great numbers, shall be avoided, I know these points are less likely to escape your attention than they would be mine. If there is anything wanting which is within my power to give, do not fail to let me know it.

And now with a brave Army, and a just cause, may God sustain you.

Yours very truly,   *A. Lincoln*

Lincoln writes to Grant requesting a position for his son Robert, recently graduated from Harvard University. Lincoln tells Grant that he, Lincoln, and not the public will pay Robert's expenses.

Executive mansion, Washington,
Jan. 19, 1865.

Lieut. General Grant:

Please read and answer this letter as though I was not President but only a friend. My son, now in his twenty second year, having graduated at Harvard, wishes to see something of the war before it ends. I do not wish to put him in the ranks, nor yet to give him a commission, to which those who have already served long, are better entitled, and better qualified to hold. Could he, without embarrassment to you, or detrimental to the service, go into your Military family with some nominal rank, I, and not the public, furnishing his necessary means? If no, say so without the least hesitation, because I am as anxious, and as deeply interested, that you shall not be encumbered as you can be yourself. Yours truly

A. Lincoln

Grant replies two days later:

...I will be most happy to have him in my Military family in the manner you propose. The nominal rank given him is immaterial but I would suggest that of Capt. as I have three

Robert Todd Lincoln, eldest of Lincoln's four children.
(National Archives)

staff officers now, of considerable service, in no higher grade.
... Please excuse my writing on a half sheet. I had no re-
source but to take the blank half of your paper.

Robert Todd Lincoln served from February 11, 1865 to June 10, 1865 on Grant's staff with the rank of captain of volunteers.

Head Quarters Armies of the United States

                                                      City Point
Lieut. General Grant.   *April. 2. 8/15 P.M. 1865.*

Allow me to tender to you, and all with you, the nations grateful thanks for this additional and magnificent success. At your kind suggestion, I think I will visit you to-morrow.

                                                 A. Lincoln

Head Quarters Armies of the United States

                                                    City Point
Lieut. General Grant   *April 7. 11 A.M. 1865*

Gen. Sheridan says "If the thing is pressed I think that Lee will surrender." Let the thing be pressed..

                                                 A. Lincoln

Lincoln invites the victorious Grant to attend a cabinet meeting in the White House on April 14, 1865. Lincoln will attend the theatre later this same evening.

Executive mansion,   *Washington,*
Lieut. Genl. Grant   *April 14, 1865*

Please call at 11. A. M. to-day instead of 9 as agreed last evening.
Yours truly   *A. Lincoln*

TROUBLE WITH POLITICIANS

... be assured, my dear sir, there are men who have "heart in it" that think you are performing your part as poorly as you think I am performing mine.

Lincoln's troubles with politicians, both from within his own party and from without, are even more legendary than his troubles with his generals. Lincoln, always the consummate pragmatist, occasionally vented his frustration as a result of the constant hammering over patronage appointments that even his closest friends displayed.

To Jesse Dubois and Ozias Hatch two of Lincoln's closest Illinois associates from his early days in Illinois politics:

> *Executive Mansion*
> *Washington, Sept. 15, 1863*

Hon. J. K. Dubois &
Hon. O. M. Hatch

> *What nation do you desire Gen. Allen to be made Quarter-Master-General of? This nation already has a Quarter-Master-General.*

> *A. Lincoln*

Not everyone, including his oldest friends, appreciated Lincoln's humor all of the time. Hatch and DuBois took offense at Lincoln's note necessitating an explanation from Lincoln.

> *Executive Mansion*
> *Washington, Sep. 22, 1863*

Hon. O. M. Hatch & Hon. J. K. Dubois:
Springfield, Ills.

> *Your letter is just received. The particular form of my despatch was jocular, which I supposed you gentlemen knew me well enough to understand. Gen. Allen is considered here as a very faithful and capable officer; and one who would be at least thought of for Quarter-Master-General if that office were vacant.*

> *A. Lincoln*

To a delegation of Kentuckians pressuring Lincoln to appoint Benjamin F. Butler to command in Kentucky:

> *You howled when Butler went to New-Orleans. Others howled when he was removed from that command. Somebody has been howling ever since at his assignment to military command. How long will it be before you, who are howling for his assignment to rule Kentucky, will be howling to me to remove him?*
> *January 2, 1865*

In this note to Stanton, Lincoln lets his frustration with military purists show. Remember, Lincoln was a frontier militia officer in the Black Hawk War in 1840 and had little appreciation for the learned strategists of classical warfare.

> *Executive Mansion*
> *Washington, Nov. 11, 1863.*
> *Hon. Secretary of War.*
> *My dear Sir:*
> *I personally wish Jacob R. Freese, of New-Jersey to be appointed a Colonel for a Colored regiment—and this regardless of whether he can tell the exact shade of Julius Caesar's hair. Yours truly*
>
> *A. Lincoln*

To Carl Schurz: Schurz, a German revolutionary, became an important part of the Republican party and support for Lincoln's election. He marshalled the support of the German-American community. Schurz became a Major General and briefly commanded the XI Army Corps before his removal in 1863. He was a constant source of advice and criticism for Lincoln throughout the war years.

> *Gen. Carl Schurz*   *Executive mansion,*
> *My dear Sir*   *Washington, Nov. 24., 1862.*
> *I have just received, and read, your letter of the 20th. The purport of it is that we lost the late elections, and the administration is failing, because the war is unsuccessful;*

and that I must not flatter myself that I am not justly to blame for it. I certainly know that if the war fails, the administration fails, and that I will be blamed for it, whether I deserve it or not. And I ought to be blamed, if I could do better. You think I could do better; and therefore you blame me already. I think I could not do better; therefore I blame you for blaming me. I understand you now to be willing to accept the help of men, who are not republicans, provided they have "heart in it." Agreed. I want no others. But who is to be the judge of hearts, or of "heart in it"? If I must discard my own judgement, and take yours, I must also take that of others; and by the time I should reject all I should be advised to reject, I should have none left, republicans, or others—not even yourself. For, be assured, my dear sir, there are men who have "heart in it" that think you are performing your part as poorly as you think I am performing mine.

A. Lincoln

Congressman Abraham Lincoln writes to his law partner back in Springfield about fellow congressman Alexander Stephens of Georgia, future vice president of the Confederacy:

Washington. Feb. 2, 1848

Dear William:
    I just take up my pen to say, that Mr. Stephens of Georgia, a little slim, pale-faced, consumptive man, with a voice like Logan's, has just concluded the very best speech, of an hour's length, I ever heard. My old withered dry eyes are full of tears yet. If he writes it out any thing like he delivered it, our people shall see a good many copies of it. Yours truly

To W H Herndon   *A. Lincoln*

BEGGING YOUR PARDON

... I am trying to evade the butchering business lately.

Of the many characteristics which personify Lincoln, few are more commonly believed than his readiness to forgive transgressions, particularly among soldiers, in issuing pardons. In civil cases Lincoln issued pardons for 375 of 456 individuals, an eighty-two percent pardon rate. Statistics are incomplete in military cases, but for the last two years of the war written pardons exist for 225 individual cases. Lincoln continually upset his generals and Secretary of War by overruling the military sentences thereby encouraging disobedience in the eyes of the military. Lincoln, however, made it clear that he could not support the execution of young boys whose major failing was their youthful inexperience nor would he support punishment which represented revenge. Clearly, Lincoln felt that enough soldiers were dying on the battlefield at the hands of the enemy, and did not want to be responsible for adding a single additional death to the growing total. Lincoln's state of mind can be best summed up in Speaker of the House Schuyler Colfax's recollection of Lincoln's comments on clemency:

> *Some of my generals complain that I impair discipline by my frequent pardons and reprieves; but it rests me after a hard day's work that I can find some excuse for saving some poor fellow's life, and I shall go to bed happy tonight as I think how joyous the signing of this name will make himself, his family and friends.*

The following telegram to General Meade sums up Lincoln's position on the question of presidential pardons for soldiers:

Washington, D.C.
Oct. 8. 1863

Major General Meade
Army of Potomac

> *I am appealed to in behalf of August Blittersdorf, at Mitchells Station, Va. to be shot to-morrow, as a deserter. I am unwilling for any boy under eighteen to be shot; and his*

father affirms that he is under sixteen.
Please answer. His Regt. or Co. not given me.

A. Lincoln

August 17, 1863

The writer of the within is reliable. Dr. Chipley has a son at Camp Chase, captured in the Confed. Army, who is now only in his eighteenth year. I think the Sec. of War may safely bail him to his father, who is unquestionably loyal.

A. Lincoln

This interesting pardon restores the soldier's pay, showing Lincoln's sensitivity to the ultimate victims of the soldier's transgression:

Aug. 17. 1863.
Executive mansion, Washington, August 12, 1863

Hon. Secretary of War: Mrs. Baird tells me that she is a widow; that her two sons and only support joined the army where one of them still is; that her other son, Isaac P. Baird, is a private in the Seventy second Pennsylvania Volunteers— Baxter's Fire Zouaves, Company K; that he is now under guard with his regiment on a charge of desertion, so that he could not take the benefit of returning under the proclamation on that subject. Please have it ascertained if this is correct, and if it is, let him be discharged from arrest and go to duty. I think, too, he should have his pay for duty actually performed. Loss of pay falls so hard upon poor families. Yours truly,

A. Lincoln

Sec of War, please see this Pittsburgh boy. He is very young, and I shall be satisfied with whatever you do with him

Aug. 21. 1863.   *A. Lincoln*

Better to restore a young soldier to the fighting ranks than to bury him underground:

To Joseph Holt
Let him fight instead of being shot.
July 18. 1863   A. Lincoln

                                                  Washington, D.C.,
                                                      Oct. 8 1863
Major General Meade
Army of Potomac

    I am appealed to in behalf of John Murphy, to be shot to-morrow. His Mother says he is but seventeen. Please answer.
                                                      A. Lincoln

Major General Meade   *Executive mansion*
Warrenton, Va   *Washington, Aug. 21, 1863.*

    At this late moment I am appealed to in behalf of William Thompson of Co. K. 3rd. Maryland Volunteers, in 12th. Army Corps said to be a deserter. He is represented to me to be very young, with symptoms of insanity. Please postpone execution till further order
                                                      A. Lincoln

Six months after his first note on behalf of Mrs. Baird's son, Lincoln writes a second note and pointedly states, *"Please do it."*

                                                  Executive Mansion
                                          Washington, March 1, 1864.
Hon. Sec. of War—
My dear Sir:
    A poor widow, by the name of Baird, has a son in the Army, that for some offence has been sentenced to serve a long time without pay, or at most, with very little pay. I do not like this punishment of withholding pay—it falls so very hard upon poor families. After he has been serving in this

way for several months, at the tearful appeal of the poor Mother, I made a direction that he be allowed to enlist for a new term, on the same conditions as others. She now comes and says she can not get it acted upon. Please do it. Yours truly

A. Lincoln

January 7, 1864

The case of Andrews is really a very bad one, as appears by the record already before me. Yet before receiving this I had ordered his punishment commuted to imprisonment for during the war at hard labor, and had so telegraphed. I did this, not on any merit in the case, but because I am trying to evade the butchering business lately.

A. Lincoln

Frequently assailed by the Christian right of his day for failing to publicly profess his faith, Lincoln shows a deeper understanding of the Christian principal of forgiveness than many of his critics.

February 5, 1864

Submitted to the Sec. of War. On principal I dislike an oath which requires a man to swear he has not done wrong. It rejects the Christian principal of forgiveness on terms of repentance. I think it is enough if the man does no wrong hereafter.

A. Lincoln

Executive Mansion
Washington, D.C. Dec. 17, 1863.
Major General Hurlbut
Memphis, Tenn.

I understand you have, under sentence of death, a tall old man, by the name of Henry F. Luckett. I personally knew him, and do not think him a bad man. Please do not let him be executed, unless upon further order from me, and, in the mean time, send me a transcript of the record.

A. Lincoln

On reviewing the record, Lincoln writes:

"Henry F. Luckett"
     Let this man, Henry F. Luckett, be pardoned, and sent North.
     March 30, 1864   *A. Lincoln*

Executive Mansion
Oct. 17, 1861

Majr. Ramsay
My dear Sir

     The lady—bearer of this—says she has two sons who want to work. Set them at it, if possible. Wanting to work is so rare a merit, that it should be encouraged. Yours truly

A. Lincoln

Major General Meade   *Washington, D.C.,*
Warrenton Va   *August 27 1863*

     Walter, Rainese, Faline, Lae, & Kuhne appeal to me for mercy, without giving any ground for it whatever. I understand these are very flagrant cases, and that you deem their punishment as being indispensable to the service. If I am not mistaken in this, please let them know at once that their appeal is denied.

A. Lincoln

The prisoners were executed on August 29, 1863 for "bounty jumping" (deserting after receiving bounty to serve as substitutes for conscripts.) They were the first to be convicted of doing so and were executed as an example to all who contemplated "bounty jumping."

Lincoln Considers the Insanity Plea.

The Case of Dr. David Minton Wright:

On July 11,1863, Second Lieutenant Anson G. Sanborn of the 1st Infantry Regiment, U.S. Color Troops was marching a company of black troops under his command down Main Street in Norfolk, Virginia when Dr. David M. Wright shot and killed him. Wright, a prominent Norfolk physician, ardent secessionist and slaveholder, was incensed at seeing black soldiers occupying his home city of Norfolk. Wright was immediately arrested and tried before a military commission. Found guilty and sentenced to death by hanging, several influential persons petitioned Lincoln on the premise that Wright was insane at the moment of the shooting. Although Wright's defense did not claim insanity, his defense attorney, Lucius H. Chandler (U.S. Attorney for the Eastern District of Virginia) sought an audience with Lincoln pleading with him to review the case. The following correspondence shows the difficulties and care Lincoln frequently went through in cases where the sentence of death was ordered. Of particular interest is Lincoln's sensitivity to the question of Wright's sanity at the time of the act.

Executive Mansion,   *Washington, August 3, 1863.*

Major General Foster, or whoever may be in command of the Military Department, with Head Quarters at Fort-Monroe, Va. If Dr. Wright, on trial at Norfolk, has been, or shall be convicted, send me a transcript of his trial and conviction, and do not let execution be done upon him, until my further order.

A. Lincoln

Major Gen. Foster   *Washington, D.C.*
Fort-Monroe,Va   *August 28, 1863*

Please notify, if you can, Mr. Segar, and Mr. Chandler, all, or any of them, that I now have the record in Dr. Wright's case, and am ready to hear them. When you shall have got the notice to them, please let me know.

A. Lincoln

After a lengthy interview, Lincoln chose Dr. John P. Gray, Superintendent of the Utica (New York) Lunatic Asylum to serve as Special Commissioner and review the case of Dr. Wright, advising Lincoln on Wright's sanity at the time of the killing.

Dr. John P. Gray   *Executive Mansion*
Washington, September 10th, 1863.

Sir:

Dr. David M. Wright is in military custody at Norfolk, Virginia, having been, by a military commission, tried for murder, and sentenced to death, his execution awaiting the order of the Major General in command of that Military Department, or of the President of the United States. The record is before me; and a question is made as to the sanity of the accused. You will please proceed to the Military Department whose head-quarters are at Fort-Monroe, and take in writing all evidence which may be offered on behalf of Dr. Wright and against him, and any, in addition, which you may find within your reach, and deem pertinent; all said evidence to be directed to the question of Dr. Wright's sanity or insanity, and not to any other questions; you to preside, with power to exclude evidence which shall appear to you clearly not pertinent to the question.

When the taking of the evidence shall be closed, you will report the same to me, together with your own conclusions, as to Dr. Wright's sanity, both at the time of the homicide, and at the time of your examination. On reaching Fort-Monroe, you will present this letter to the officer then commanding that Department, and deliver to him a copy of the same; upon which he is hereby directed to notify Hon. L. J. Bowden, and Hon. L.H. Chandler, of the same; to designate some suitable person in his command to appear for the government, as Judge Advocate or Prosecuting Attorney; to provide for the attendance of all such witnesses before you as may be desired by either party, or by yourself, and who may be within convenient reach of you; to furnish you a suitable place, or places for conducting the examination; and to render you such other reasonable assistance in the premises as you may require. If you deem it proper, you will examine Dr. Wright personally, and you may, in your discretion, require him to be present during the whole, or any part, of the taking of evidence. The Military are hereby charged to see that an escape does not occur. Yours truly.

A. Lincoln

Dr. John P. Gray.   *Executive mansion,*
Norfolk, Va.   *Washington, Sept. 13, 1863.*

The names of those whose affidavits are left with me on the question of Dr. Wright's sanity are as follows:

Mrs. Jane C. Bolsom   *Mrs. Elizabeth Rooks.*
Mrs. M.E. Smiley   *Dr. E.D. Granier*
Moses Hudgin   *Thomas K. Murray*
J.D. Ghislin, Jr.   *William J. Holmes*
Felix Logue   *Miss Margaret E. Wigeon*
Robert B. Tunstall, M.D   *Mrs. Emily S. Frost*

A. Lincoln

Following his examination of Wright, Dr. Gray reported back to Lincoln, "I am of the opinion that Doctor David M. Wright was not insane prior to the 11th day of July, 1863, the date of the homicide of Lieutenant Sanborn; and that he has not been insane since, and is not insane now."

October 7, 1863

Upon the presentation of the record in this case and the examination thereof, aided by the report thereon of the Judge-Advocate-General, and on full hearing of the counsel for the accused, being satisfied that no proper question remained open except as to the insanity of the accused, I caused a very full examination to be made on that question, upon a great amount of evidence, including all offered by counsel of accused, by an expert of high reputation in that professional department, who thereon reports to me, as his opinion, that the accused Dr. David M. Wright, was not insane prior to or on the 11th day of July, 1863, the date of the homicide of Lieutenant Sanborn; that he has not been insane since, and is not insane now (October 7, 1863). I therefore approve the finding and sentence of the military commission, and direct that the major-general in command of the department including the place of trial, and wherein the convict is now in custody, appoint time and place and carry said sentence into execution.

Abraham Lincoln

Washington, D.C.,
Oct. 15 1863

Major General Foster
Fort-Monroe, Va

Postpone the execution of Dr. Wright to Friday the 23rd. Inst. This is intended for his preparation and is final.

A. Lincoln

Washington, D.C.
Oct. 17. 1863

Major General Foster
Fort-Monroe, Va

It would be useless for Mrs. Dr. Wright to come here. The subject is a very painful one, but the case is settled.

A. Lincoln

Dr. David M. Wright was executed on October 23, 1863 pursuant to Lincoln upholding the findings of the Military Commission. Wright's family was allowed to leave Union occupied Norfolk and moved to Confederate-held Petersburg, Virginia. On March 10, 1864, the Confederate General Assembly of Virginia passed a resolution honoring Dr. David M. Wright for his "martyred death."

Lincoln Personally Frees the Nephew of Confederate Vice President Alexander H. Stephens:

John A. Stephens, nephew of Confederate Vice President Alexander H. Stephens, enlisted as a private in the First Georgia Regulars in September, 1861. In April 1862, he transferred to the Confederate Signal Service as a First Lieutenant and was assigned to Port Hudson, Louisiana where he was taken prisoner when that bastion fell to General Nathaniel Banks on July 9, 1863. Stephens eventually wound up being confined at the officer's prison at Johnson's Island in Lake Erie. Following his capture at Port Hudson, Stephens dropped from sight from his family who lost all contact or knowledge of his whereabouts or whether he was even alive. Alexander Stephens appealed to Lincoln, his fellow congressman from 1847 to 1849, for help in locating his nephew. On February 5, 1865, Lt. Stephens was ordered to the commandant's office where he was shown a telegram which read:

Alexander H. Stephens. *(National Archives)*

Washington, D.C.,   February 4, 1865

Officer in command at Johnson's Island, Ohio: Parole Lieutenant John A. Stephens, prisoner of war, to report to me here in person, and send him to me. It is in pursuance of an arrangement I made yesterday with his uncle, Hon. A. H. Stephens. Acknowledge receipt.

A. Lincoln

Arriving at the White House several days later, Stephens tells of being led into Lincoln's office where he found the president lying full length on a table with his head resting on his hand talking to Secretary of State William Seward who was sitting in a chair opposite Lincoln. After chatting with Stephens about his uncle, Lincoln penned the following letter which he gave to Stephens and asked him to give it to his uncle:

Lieutenant John A. Stephens, CSA, nephew of Confederate vice-president Alexander H. Stephens. *(Lincoln Herald, June, 1943)*

Executive Mansion,   *Washington, Feb. 10, 1865*

Hon. A. H. Stephens

    According to our agreement your nephew, Lieut. Stephens, goes to you bearing this note. Please, in return, to select and send to me that officer of the same rank imprisoned at Richmond whose physical condition most urgently requires his release.

      Respectfully,   *A. Lincoln*

Lincoln also handed Stephens a carte de visite photograph of himself which he signed, *A. Lincoln*, stating:

    Suppose you take this along with you. I don't expect there are many of them down south.

By the time Stephens arrived in Richmond Lincoln was dead and his uncle arrested as a political prisoner. Alexander Stephens was released in October, 1865, and eventually returned to Congress. John Stephens became a successful lawyer in Georgia serving as Adjutant General of Georgia. Both the letter and signed photograph hung on the wall of the Stephens home in a special place of honor.

Socks

I accept them ...as an evidence, of the patriotic devotion which, at your advanced age, you bear to our just and great cause.

Socks you say? Why socks? Nothing was too small or too trivial for Lincoln. Lincoln's softest spot was for little old gray-haired ladies who could be found rocking by a crackling hearth in rural America. He was ever mindful of his own roots and the people who surrounded him in his early years. The following letters were as important to Lincoln as many that concerned affairs of state. They include letters about his feet which caused him considerable trouble at times.

Executive Mansion
Washington, May 5, 1864.

Mrs. Abner Bartlett

My dear Madam.
I have received the very excellent pair of socks of your own knitting, which you did me the honor to send. I accept them as a very comfortable article to wear; but more gratefully as an evidence, of the patriotic devotion which, at your advanced age, you bear to our great and just cause.
May God give you yet many happy days. Yours truly

A. Lincoln

Executive Mansion
Washington Jany 8, 1864

Mrs. Esther Stockton.
Madam: Learning that you who have passed the eighty-fourth year of life, have given to the soldiers, some three hundred pairs of stockings, knitted by yourself, I wish to offer my thanks. You will also convey my thanks, to those young ladies who have done so much in feeding our soldiers while passing through your city? Yours truly,

A. Lincoln

Executive Mansion,
Washington, Dec. 4, 1861

My dear Madam
I take great pleasure in acknowledging the receipt of your letter of Nov. 26; and in thanking you for the present by which it was accompanied. A pair of socks, so fine, and soft, and warm, could hardly have been manufactured in any other way than the old Kentucky fashion. Your letter informs me that your maiden name was Crume, and that you were raised in Washington county, Kentucky, by which I infer that an uncle of mine by marriage was a relative of yours. Nearly, or quite sixty years ago, Ralph Crume married Mary Lincoln, a

sister of my father, in Washington county, Kentucky.
Accept my thanks, and believe me, Very truly your Friend

A. Lincoln

While the following note is not about Lincoln's socks, it is about the closest thing to them, his feet:

Dr. Zacharie has operated on my feet with great success, and considerable addition to my comfort.

A. Lincoln

Sep. 22.1862.

Dr. Isachar Zacharie was a chiropodist who sought and widely used testimonials from many of the president's cabinet members as well as the president. It seems singularly peculiar to us today that such distinguished persons would allow themselves to be used for such commercial purposes. It was not uncommon, however, and Lincoln cheerfully complied.

LINCOLN AND THE UNION

We shall nobly save or meanly lose, the last best hope of earth.

From a letter to James C. Conkling regarding Illinois Unionists:

Hon. James C. Conkling   *Executive Mansion*
Washington, August 26, 1863

My Dear Sir.
...There are those who are dissatisfied with me. To such I would say: You desire peace; and you blame me that we do not have it. But how can we attain it? There are but three conceivable ways. First, to suppress the rebellion by force of arms. This I am trying to do. Are you for it? If you are, so far we are agreed. If you are not for it, a second way is, to

give up the Union. I am against this. Are you for it? If you are, you should say so plainly. If you are not for force, nor yet for dissolution, there only remains some imaginable compromise. I do not believe any compromise embracing the maintenance of the Union, is now possible. All I learn, leads to a directly opposite belief. The strength of the rebellion, is its military—its army. That army dominates all the country, and all the people, within its range. Any offer of terms made by any man or men within that range, in opposition to that army, is simply nothing for the present; because such man or men, have no power whatever to enforce their side of a compromise, if one were made with them. To illustrate—suppose refugees from the South, and peace men of the North, get together in convention, and frame and proclaim a compromise embracing a restoration of the Union; in what way can that compromise be used to keep Lee's army out of Pennsylvania? Meade's army can keep Lee's army out of Pennsylvania; and, I think, can ultimately drive it out of existence. But no paper compromise, to which the controllers of Lee's army are not agreed, can, at all, affect that army. In an effort at such compromise we should waste time, which the enemy would improve to our disadvantage; and that would be all. A compromise, to be effective, must be made with either those who control the rebel army, or with the people first liberated from the domination of that army, by the success of our own army.

Horace Greeley (1811–1872), was editor of the *New York Tribune*. Lincoln's famous letter to Greeley was written in response to an editorial entitled, "Prayer to Twenty Millions," which harshly chastised Lincoln for his seeming lack of support for emancipation. Lincoln felt compelled to answer Greeley's editorial and sent him the following letter. It is often quoted in part against Lincoln to suggest that he had no interest at all in emancipation and was essentially a hypocrite when it came to black freedom. Lincoln's closing sentence, which is never quoted by his critics, belies the idea that he was not consistent in his views on emancipation.

Horace Greeley, Editor of the New York Times.
(Author's collection)

Hon. Horace Greely: *Executive mansion,*
                              Washington, August 22, 1862.
Dear Sir:
    *I have just read yours of the 19th. addressed to myself
through the New York Tribune. If there be in it any state-
ments, or assumptions of fact, which I may know to be erro-
neous, I do not, now and here, controvert them. If there be in
it any inferences which I may believe to be falsely drawn, I do
not now and here, argue against them. If there be perceptible
in it an impatient and dictatorial tone, I waive it in deference
to an old friend, whose heart I have always supposed to be
right.*
    *As to the policy I "seem to be pursuing" as you say, I
have not meant to leave anyone in doubt.*

I would save the Union. I would save it the shortest way under the Constitution. The sooner the national authority can be restored; the nearer the Union will be "the Union as it was." If there be those who would not save the Union, unless they could at the same time save slavery, I do not agree with them. If there be those who would not save the Union unless at the same time destroy slavery, I do not agree with them. My paramount object in this struggle is to save the Union, and is not either to save or destroy slavery. If I could save the Union without freeing any slave I would do it, and if I could save it by freeing all the slaves I would do it; and if I could save it by freeing some and leaving others alone I would also do that. What I do about slavery, and the colored race, I do because I believe it helps to save the Union; and what I forbear, I forbear because I do not believe it would help to save the Union. I shall do less whenever I shall believe what I am doing hurts the cause, and I shall do more whenever I shall believe doing more will help the cause. I shall try to correct errors when shown to be errors; and I shall adopt new views so fast as they shall appear to be true views.

*I have here stated my purpose according to my view of official duty; and **I intend no modification of my oft-expressed personal wish that all men every where could be free*** (emphasis added). *Yours,*

A. Lincoln

From Lincoln's Annual Message to Congress, December 1, 1862:

*We say we are for the Union. The world will not forget that we say this. We know how to save the Union. The world knows we do know how to save it. We—even we here—hold the power, and bear the responsibility. In giving freedom to the slave, we assure freedom to the free—honorable alike in what we give, and what we preserve. **We shall nobly save, or meanly lose, the last best hope of earth.***

EMANCIPATION

...You say you will not fight to free negroes. Some of them seem to be willing to fight for you;...

On January 1, 1863, the Emancipation Proclamation, issued preliminarily on September 22, 1862, took effect officially. In simplest terms it declared that all persons held as slaves within states or parts of states still in rebellion against the United States on January 1, 1863, were henceforward and forever free.

It was received by many people, both North and South, with derision and vitriol. Many claimed it was a cheap trick which, in reality, freed no one. While certain persons have characterized it as a base, political hoax issued for pure political advantage, its issuance actually cost Lincoln dearly in the fall elections of 1862. In addition, the stock market fell and enlistments dropped off precipitously in certain parts of the North. Its issuance was anything but politically motivated. In England, the British government reacted with what can only be described as abhorrence.

To Lincoln's relief, however, the working people of England rallied to his side with a show of support completely unexpected. The textile mills of England were seriously crippled by the blockade and the war. Thousands of workers were put out of work as the supply of cotton was severely curtailed. Imagine, then, the wonder of the letter which Lincoln received on January 2, 1863, from the workingmen of Manchester, England which read in part: "We joyfully honor you, as President, and the Congress with you, for the many decisive steps toward practically exemplifying your belief in the words of your great founders, 'All men are created free and equal.' Accept our high admiration of your firmness in upholding the proclamation of freedom."

Lincoln happily responds:

To the workingmen of Manchester: *January 19, 1863.*

...I cannot but regard your decisive utterance upon the question (of emancipation) as an instance of sublime Chris-

tian heroism which has not been surpassed in any age or in any country. It is indeed, an energetic and reinspiring assurance of the inherent power of truth and of the ultimate and universal triumph of justice, humanity, and freedom. I do not doubt that the sentiments you have expressed will be sustained by your great nation, and, on the other hand, I have no hesitation in assuring you that they will excite admiration, esteem, and the most reciprocal feelings of friendship among the American people. I hail this interchange of sentiment, therefore, as an augury that, whatever else may happen, whatever misfortune may befall your country or my own, the peace and friendship which now exist between the two nations will be, as it shall be my desire to make them, perpetual.

Abraham Lincoln

James C. Conkling was a close friend and political associate of Lincoln in Springfield, Illinois. Conkling was Mayor of Springfield in 1844 and was elected a member of the Illinois House of Representatives in 1851. The following excerpt is in response to an invitation from Conkling to Lincoln to speak before a large Union rally in Illinois in August, 1863. Lincoln declined to attend, but wrote a letter to Conkling which he asked Conkling to read to the assembled delegates. Lincoln wrote in his letter to Conkling, "you are one of the best public readers," but asked him to "read it very slowly." Lincoln did not want his audience to miss any part of his carefully worded statement.

Hon. James C. Conkling   *Executive mansion*
Washington, August 26, 1863.

...But, to be plain, you are dissatisfied with me about the negro. Quite likely there is a difference of opinion between you and myself upon that subject. I certainly wish that all men could be free, while I suppose you do not. Yet I have neither adopted, nor proposed any measure, which is not consistent with even your view, provided you are for the Union. I suggested compensated emancipation; to which you replied

you wished not to be taxed to buy negroes. But I had not asked you to be taxed to buy negroes, except in such way, as to save you from greater taxation to save the Union exclusively by other means.

You dislike the emancipation proclamation; and perhaps would have it retracted. You say it is unconstitutional—I think differently. I think the constitution invests its commander-in-chief, with the law of war, in time of war. The most that can be said, if so much is, that slaves are property. Is there—has there ever been—any question that by the law of war, property, both of enemies and friends, may be taken when needed? And is it not needed whenever taking it, helps us, or hurts the enemy? Armies, the world over, destroy the enemies' property when they can not use it; and even destroy their own to keep it from the enemy. Civilized belligerents do all in their power to help themselves, or hurt the enemy, except a few things regarded as barbarous or cruel. Among the exceptions are the massacre of vanquished foes, and non-combatants, male and female.

...You say you will not fight to free negroes. Some of them seem to be willing to fight for you; but, no matter. Fight you, then, exclusively to save the Union. I issued the proclamation on purpose to aid you in saving the Union. Whenever you shall have conquered all resistance to the Union, I shall urge you to continue fighting, it will be an apt time, then, for you to declare you will not fight to free negroes.

I thought that in your struggle for the Union, to whatever extent the negroes should cease helping the enemy, to that extent it weakened the enemy in his resistance to you. Do you think differently? I thought that whatever negroes can be got to do as soldiers, leaves just so much less for white soldiers to do, in saving the Union. Does it appear otherwise to you? But negroes, like other people, act upon motives. Why should they do anything for us, if we will do nothing for them? If they stake their lives for us, they must be prompted by the strongest motive—even the promise of freedom. And the promise being made, must be kept.

To Salmon P. Chase, Secretary of the Treasury:

Hon. S. P. Chase   *Executive Mansion,*
Washington, September 2, 1863.
My dear Sir:

    Knowing your great anxiety that the emancipation proc-
lamation shall now be applied to certain parts of Virginia
and Louisiana which were exempted from it last January, I
state briefly what appear to me to be difficulties in the way of
such a step. The original proclamation has no constitutional
or legal justification, except as a military measure. The ex-
emptions were made because the military necessity did not
apply to the exempted localities. Nor does that necessity ap-
ply to them now any more than it did then. If I take the step
must I not do so, without the argument of military necessity,
and so, without any argument, except the one that I think the
measure politically expedient, and morally right? Would I
not thus give up all footing upon constitution or law? Would
I not thus be in the boundless field of absolutism? Could this
pass unnoticed or unresisted? Could it fail to be perceived
that without any further stretch, I might do the same in Dela-
ware, Maryland, Kentucky, Tennessee, and Missouri; and even
change any law in any state? Would not many of our own
friends shrink away appalled? Would it not lose us the elec-
tions, and with them, the very cause we seek to advance?

Lincoln contributes to the relief and comfort of the soldier:

Executive mansion, Washington,
Oct. 26. 1863.
Ladies having in charge of the North-Western Fair
For the Sanitary Commission Chicago, Illinois

    According to your request made in your behalf, the origi-
nal draft of the Emancipation proclamation is herewith en-
closed. The formal words at the top, and the conclusion,
except the signature, you perceive, are not in my hand-writing.
They were written at the State Department by whom I know
not. The printed part was cut from a copy of the preliminary
proclamation, and pasted on merely to save writing.

*I had some desire to retain the paper; but if it shall con-
tribute to the relief or comfort of the soldiers that will be
better. Your obt. Servt.*

A. Lincoln

The Sanitary Commission, a beneficient organization similar to the Red Cross of later years, provided a variety of services
and help to Union soldiers both in rest areas and in the field.
The original draft was sold at the fair to Thomas B. Bryan who
presented it to the Soldiers' Home in Chicago. It was eventually
produced as a lithograph and copies sold to raise funds for the
Soldiers' Home. The original manuscript was destroyed in the
Chicago fire of 1871.

...ALL MEN ARE CREATED EQUAL

*I am a living witness that any one of your children may look to
come here as my father's child has.*

The question of equality is central to the Lincoln theme.
Interestingly, Lincoln's standard or well-spring for American
democracy was the Declaration of Independence as opposed to
the Constitution. Consider the Gettysburg Address in which
Lincoln measures the date "... our fathers brought forth upon
this continent a new birth of freedom." That moment in our
history was "Four score and seven years ago...," or 1776, not
1787, the date of our Constitution. Lincoln often referred to the
famous phrase which stated that all men were created equal
and just as often, explained what that meant to him and what
that should mean to others. In his writings on equality, we can
see more clearly Lincoln's ideas of freedom and equality—for
all. The following quotes from Lincoln are the very soul of his
character and set him apart from many of his contemporaries.
From notes, September 16, 1858:

*I believe the declaration that "all men are created equal"
is the great fundamental principal upon which our free insti-
tutions rest. That negro slavery is violative of that principal.*

From the first debate with Stephen A. Douglas at Ottawa, Illinois, August 21, 1858:

> *...There is no reason in the world why the negro is not entitled to all the natural rights enumerated in the Declaration of Independence, the right to life, liberty and the pursuit of happiness. I hold that he is as much entitled to these as the white man. I agree with Judge Douglas he is not my equal in many respects—certainly not in color, perhaps not in moral or intellectual endowment. But in the right to eat the bread, without leave of anybody else, which his own hand earns, he is my equal and the equal of Judge Douglas, and the equal of every living man.*

From notes on slavery believed dated July 1, 1854:

> *Most governments have been based, practically, on the denial of equal rights of men, as I have, in part, stated them; ours began, by affirming those rights. They said, some men are too ignorant, and vicious, to share in government. Possibly so, said we; and, by your system, you would always keep them ignorant and vicious. We proposed to give all a chance; and we expected the weak to grow stronger, the ignorant, wiser; and all better, and happier together.*
>
> *...As labor is the common burden of our race, so the effort of some to shift their share of the burden onto the shoulders of others is the great durable curse of the race.*

Speech at Chicago, Illinois, July 10, 1858:

> *My friends, I have detained you about as long as I desired to do, and I have only to say, let us discard all this quibbling about this man and the other man—this race and that race and the other race being inferior, and therefore they must be placed in an inferior position—discarding our standard that we have left us. Let us discard all these things, and unite as one people throughout this land, until we shall once more stand up declaring that all men are created equal.*

From a speech delivered at Springfield, Illinois, June 26, 1857, in response to Stephen A. Douglas' attacks on Lincoln's position that negroes are included in the Declaration of Independence:

> ...*Now I protest against that counterfeit logic which concludes that, because I do not want a black woman for a slave I must necessarily want her for a wife. I need not have her for either, I can just leave her alone. In some respects she certainly is not my equal; but in her natural right to eat the bread she earns with her own hands without asking leave of anyone else, she is my equal, and the equal of all others.*

Address at Gettysburg, Pennsylvania dedicating a National Cemetery:

> *November 19, 1863*
> > *Executive mansion, Washington.*

> *Four score and seven years ago our fathers brought forth, upon this continent, a new nation, conceived in liberty, and dedicated to the proposition that "all men are created equal."*

From a speech to the 164th Ohio Volunteer Infantry, August 22, 1864:

> *...I happen temporarily to occupy this big White House. I am a living witness that any one of your children may look to come here as my father's child has. It is in order that each of you may have through this free government which we have enjoyed, an open field and a fair chance for your industry, enterprise and intelligence; that you may all have equal privileges* (sic) *in the race of life, with all of its desirable human aspirations.*

Oft remembered, most quoted

The fiery trial through which we pass, will light us down, in honor or dishonor, to the latest generation.

When Lincoln is at his best, his writings take on a prose-like quality which holds the reader tightly. The precision of his mind did not in any way dim his mastery of written expression. Here is a sampling of his finer examples of writing.

From Lincoln's Annual Message to the Congress, December 1, 1862:

> ...*The dogmas of the quiet past, are inadequate to the stormy present. The occasion is piled high with difficulty, and we must rise with the occasion. As our case is new, so we must think anew, and act anew. We must disenthrall ourselves, and then we shall save our country.*

And further:

> *Fellow-citizens, we cannot escape history. We of this Congress and this administration, will be remembered in spite of ourselves. No personal significance, or insignificance, can spare one or another of us. The fiery trial through which we pass, will light us down, in honor or dishonor, to the latest generation.*

From the Second Inaugural Address, March 4, 1865:

> *With malice toward none; with charity for all; with firmness in the right as God gives us to see the right, let us strive on to finish the work we are in; to bind up the nation's wounds; to care for him who shall have borne the battle, and for his widow, and his orphan—to do all which may achieve and cherish a just, and a lasting peace, among ourselves, and with all nations.*

On February 11, 1861, Lincoln prepared to board a train that would be the first in a long route throughout the northern states on his ride to Washington to assume the presidency. Lincoln left from the old Western Railroad terminal in Springfield where a large crowd of fellow neighbors had gathered in a light rainfall to see him off. Most accounts accept that Lincoln spoke to the crowd extemporaneously, at least not from written notes, the short, moving farewell that appears here. The

> *With malice toward none; with charity for all; with firmness in the right, as God gives us to see the right, let us strive on to finish the work we are in; to bind up the nation's wounds; to care for him who shall have borne the battle, and for his widow, and his orphan—to do all which may achieve and cherish a just, and a lasting peace, among ourselves, and with all nations.*

Closing paragraph of Lincoln's Second Inaugural Address.
(Library of Congress)

National Cathedral in Washington, D.C. has dedicated one of two bays to Lincoln. A committee of Lincoln scholars, appointed by the church directors, chose Lincoln's farewell speech to be memorialized in marble in the bay along with a magnificent heroic bronze statue by Walter Hancock.

> *My friends: No one, not in my situation, can appreciate my feeling of sadness at this parting. To this place, and the kindness of these people, I owe everything. Here I have lived a quarter of a century, and have passed from a young to an old man. Here my children have been born, and one is buried. I now leave, not knowing when or whether ever I may return, with a task before me greater than that which rested upon Washington. Without the assistance of that Divine Being who ever attended him, I cannot succeed. With that assistance, I cannot fail. Trusting in Him who can go with me, and remain with you, and be everywhere for good, let us confidently hope that all will yet be well. To His care commending you, as I hope in your prayers you will commend me, I bid you an affectionate farewell.*

One of Lincoln's more famous letters was written to a young girl named Grace Bedell. On October 15, 1860, in the midst of the presidential campaign, the young girl from upstate New York wrote the candidate a letter in which she offered the would-be president some political advice: *"I have got four brothers and part of them will vote for you anyway and if you let your whiskers grow I will try and get the rest of them to vote for you; you would look a great deal better for your face is so thin."* Four days later, On October 19, Lincoln responds in characteristic style:

Private

Springfield, Ills.
Oct 19. 1860

Miss. Grace Bedell

My dear little Miss.

Your very agreeable letter of the 15th. is received. I regret the necessity of saying I have no daughters. I have three sons—one seventeen, one nine, and one seven, years of age. They, with their mother, constitute my whole family.

As to the whiskers, having never worn any, do you not think people would call it a piece of silly affec(ta)tion if I were to begin it now? Your very sincere well wisher

A. Lincoln

Grace Bedell Billings.
(Author's collection)

GETTYSBURG—THE BATTLE

...my dear general, I do not believe you appreciate the magnitude of the misfortune involved in Lee's escape.

Press Release

Washington City, July 4, 10. A.M. 1863

The President announces to the country that news from the Army of the Potomac, up to 10 P.M. of the 3rd. is such as to cover that Army with the highest honor, to promise a great success to the cause of the Union, and to claim the condolence of all for the many gallant fallen. And that for this, he especially desires that on this day, He whose will, not ours, should ever be done, be everywhere remembered and reverenced with profoundest gratitude.

Abraham Lincoln

To Henry W. Halleck who served as General-in-Chief until his official replacement by Ullyses S. Grant in March, 1864:

Major-General Halleck: *July 7, 1863*

We have certain information that Vicksburg surrendered to General Grant on the 4th of July. Now if General Meade can complete his work, so gloriously prosecuted thus far, by the literal or substantial destruction of Lee's army, the rebellion will be over. Yours truly,

A. Lincoln

Halleck sent a dispatch to General George Gorden Meade, Commanding the Army of the Potomac, on July 14, 1863, in which he said in part:

"...I need hardly say to you that the escape of Lee's army without another battle has created great dissatisfaction in the mind of the President, and it will require an active and energetic pursuit on your part to remove the impression that it has not been sufficiently active heretofore."

Meade telegraphs back to Halleck on the same day:

"Having performed my duty conscientiously and to the best of my ability, the censure of the President conveyed in your dispatch of 1 p.m. this day, is, in my judgement, so undeserved that I feel compelled most respectfully to be asked to be immediately relieved from the command of this army."

Lincoln had become convinced that by not quickly following up against Lee while he was pinned against the Potomac River, Meade had willingly lost the obvious opportunity to completely smash Lee's army and finally end the war. Lincoln remained deeply depressed for several days. Now he felt compelled to explain to Meade his feelings in such a way as to ameliorate Meade's position without compromising his own. Lincoln writes the following letter to Meade which was neither sent nor signed:

Executive mansion,
Major General Meade   *Washington, July 14, 1863.*

I have just seen your dispatch to Gen. Halleck, asking to be relieved of your command, because of a supposed censure of mine. I am very—very—grateful to you for the magnificent success you gave the cause of the country at Gettysburg; and I am sorry now to be the author of the slightest pain to you. But I was in such deep distress myself that I could not restrain some expression of it. I had been oppressed nearly ever since the battles at Gettysburg, by what appeared to be evidences that yourself, and Gen. Couch, and Gen. Smith, were not seeking a collision with the enemy, but were trying to get him across the river without another battle. What these evidences were, if you please, I hope to tell you at some time, when we shall both feel better. The case, summarily stated is this. You fought and beat the enemy at Gettysburg; and, of course, to say the least, his loss was as great as yours. He retreated; you did not, as it seemed to me, pressingly pursue him; but a flood in the river detained him, till, by slow degrees, you were again upon him. You had at least twenty thousand veteran troops directly with you, and as many more raw ones within supporting distance, all in addition to those who fought with you at Gettysburg; while it was not possible that he had received a single recruit; and yet you stood and let the flood run down, bridges be built, and the enemy move away at his leisure, without attacking him.

...Again, my dear general, I do not believe you appreciate the magnitude of the misfortune involved in Lee's escape. He was within your easy grasp, and to have closed upon him would, in connection with our other late successes, have ended the war. As it is, the war will be prolonged indefinitely. If you could not safely attack Lee last Monday, how can you possibly do so south of the river, when you can take with you very few more than two thirds of the force you then had in hand? It would be unreasonable to expect, and I do not expect you can now effect much. Your golden opportunity is gone, and I am distressed immeasurably because of it.

I beg you will not consider this a prosecution, or persecution of yourself. As you had learned that I was dissatisfied, I have thought it best to kindly tell you why.

To Oliver O. Howard, commanding general of the Eleventh Army Corps at Gettysburg: Howard was a close friend of Lincoln and a principal in the establishment of the Lincoln Memorial University in Harrowgate, Tennessee. By the date of this letter, Lincoln has begun to recover from his depression at what might have been.

Executive mansion,
Washington, July 21. 1863.

My dear General Howard

Your letter of the 18th is received. I was deeply mortified by the escape of Lee across the Potomac, because the substantial destruction of his army would have ended the war, and because I believed, such destruction was perfectly easy— believed that Gen. Meade and his noble army had expended all the skill, and toil, and blood, up to the ripe harvest, and then let the crop go to waste. ...A few days having past, I am now profoundly grateful for what was done, without criticism for what was not done. Gen. Meade has my confidence as a brave and skillful officer, and a true man. Yours very truly

A. Lincoln

GETTYSBURG—THE DEDICATION

*I am pleased to know that, in your judgement, the little I did
say was not entirely a failure.*

To Stephen T. Logan: Lincoln was an earlier law partner of
Logan's in Springfield. Ward Hill Lamon was among Lincoln's
inner circle of Illinois friends and confidants and was appointed
Marshall of the District of Columbia by Lincoln. He had been
asked by the Gettysburg committee to serve as Grand Marshall
of the ceremonies. He was also Logan's son-in-law.

*Executive mansion,
Washington, Nov. 9, 1863.*

Dear Judge

*Col. Lamon had made his calculation, as he tells me, to
go to Illinois and bring Mrs. L. home this month, when he
was called on to act as Marshall on the occasion of dedicating the Cemetery at Gettysburg Pa on the 19th. He came to
me, and I told him I thought that in view of his relationship to
the government and to me, he could not well decline. Now,
why would it not be pleasant for you to come on with Mrs. L.
at the same time?*

*It will be an interesting ceremony, and I shall be very
glad to see you. I know not whether you would care to remain
to the meeting of congress, but that event, as you know, will
be very near at hand. Your friend as ever*

A. Lincoln

To Salmon P. Chase, Secretary of the Treasury:

*Hon. Secretary of the Treasury   Executive mansion,
Washington, Nov. 17, 1863.*

My dear Sir:

*I expected to see you here at Cabinet meeting, and to say
something about going to Gettysburg. There will be a train
to take and return us. The time for starting is not yet fixed;
but when it shall be, I will notify you. Yours truly*

A. Lincoln

***Ward Hill Lamon. Grand Marshal of the
Gettysburg ceremonies.*** *(Author's collection)*

To Edwin M. Stanton, Secretary of War and in charge of the
Military Railroad: Stanton had arranged for a military train to
take Lincoln to and from Gettysburg. Stanton had scheduled
the special train to leave on the morning of the 19th and arrive
just prior to the ceremonies. Lincoln felt strongly about the
importance of the dedication and not missing any part of it.

November 17, 1863.

> *I do not like this arrangement. I do not wish to so go that
> by the slightest accident we fail entirely, and, at the best, the
> whole to be a mere breathless running of the gauntlet. But,
> any way.*
>
> A. Lincoln

The President's Address: There are five accepted copies of
the address in Lincoln's handwriting. The text presented here
is from the second draft, believed to represent the version he
spoke at the ceremonies.

Four Score and seven years ago our fathers brought forth, upon this continent, a new nation, conceived in Liberty, and dedicated to the proposition that all men are created equal.

Now we are engaged in a great civil war, testing whether that nation, or any nation, so conceived, and so dedicated, can long endure. We are met here on a great battle-field of that war. We have come to dedicate a portion of it as a final resting place for those who here gave their lives that that nation might live. It is altogether fitting and proper that we should do this.

But in a larger sense we can not dedicate—we can not consecrate—we can not hallow this ground. The brave men, living and dead, who struggled here, have consecrated it far above our poor power to add or detract. The world will little note nor long remember, what we say here, but can never forget what they did here. It is for us, the living, rather to be dedicated here to the unfinished work which they have, thus far, so nobly carried on. It is rather for us to be here dedicated to the great task remaining before us—that from these honored dead we take increased devotion to that cause for which they here gave the last full measure of devotion—that we here highly resolve that these dead shall not have died in vain; that this nation shall have a new birth of freedom; and that this government of the people, by the people, for the people, shall not perish from the earth.

On November 20, 1863, Edward Everett wrote to Lincoln and stated in part:

"...I should be glad, if I could flatter myself that I came as near to the central idea of the occasion, in two hours, as you did in two minutes."

Hon. Edward Everett.   *Executive mansion,*
                                          Washington, Nov. 20, 1863.
My dear Sir:
Your kind note of to-day is received. In our respective parts yesterday, you could not have been excused to make a short address, nor I a long one. I am pleased to know that, in your judgement, the little I did say was not entirely a failure.... Your Obt. Servt.

                                          A. Lincoln

LINCOLN AND THE LAW

As a peacemaker the lawyer has a superior opportunity of being a good man.

Advice to would-be lawyers:

...resolve to be honest at all events; and if in your own judgement you can not be an honest lawyer, resolve to be honest without being a lawyer. Choose some other occupation, rather than one in the choosing of which you do, in advance, consent to be a knave.

Not a high-priced man. Lincoln's ethic shows through:

Mr. George P. Floyd,   *Springfield, Illinois*
Quincy, Illinois.   *February 21, 1856.*

Dear Sir: I have just received yours of 16th, with check on Flagg & Savage for twenty-five dollars. You must think I am a high-priced man. You are too liberal with your money.
Fifteen dollars is enough for the job. I send you a receipt for fifteen dollars, and return to you a ten-dollar bill. Yours truly,

A. Lincoln

Lincoln gives his countrymen a credo to live by. From a speech delivered in Springfield, Illinois, January 27, 1837:

Let reverence for the laws be breathed by every American mother to the lisping babe that prattles on her lap; let it be taught in the schools, seminaries, and in colleges; let it be written in primers, spelling books, and in almanacs; let it be preached from the pulpit, proclaimed in legislative halls, and enforced in courts of justice. And, in short, let it become the political religion of the nation....
... and let the old and young, the rich and the poor, the grave and the gay of all sexes and tongues and colors and conditions, sacrifice unceasingly upon its altars.

Notes for a lecture on law, July 1, 1850:

I am not an accomplished lawyer. I find as much material for a lecture in those points wherein I have failed, as in those wherein I have been moderately successful.

...Discourage litigation. Persuade your neighbors to compromise whenever you can. Point out to them how the nominal winner is often a real loser—in fees, expenses, and waste of time. As a peacemaker the lawyer has a superior opportunity of being a good man. There will still be business enough.

On long legal briefs Lincoln wrote:

It's like the lazy preacher that used to write long sermons, and the explanation was, he got to writin' and was too lazy to stop.

THE FAIRER SEX

She is a saucy woman...

From a letter to Mrs. Orville H. Browning: Lincoln wrote to his good friend, Mrs. Browning, after Mary Owens rejected his proposal.

Springfield, April 1, 1838

...Others have been made fools of by the girls; but this can never be with truth said of me. I most emphatically, in this instance, made a fool of myself. I have now come to the conclusion never again to think of marrying; and for this reason; I can never be satisfied with anyone to be block head enough to have me.

Brief remarks at Utica, N.Y. while en route to Washington, D.C. for his inauguration on March 4, 1861:

Mary Owens, who rejected Lincoln's proposal of marriage.
(Illinois State Historical Society)

February 18, 1861.

I appear before you to bid you farewell—to see you, and to allow you all to see me. At the same time I acknowledge, ladies, that I think I have the best of the bargain in the sight.

A. Lincoln

Executive Mansion,   *Washington. Aug. 23, 1862.*

To-day, Mrs. Major Paul, of the Regular Army calls and urges the appointment of her husband as a Brig. Genl. She is a saucy woman and I am afraid she will keep tormenting till I may have to do it.

A. Lincoln

Mrs. Paul succeeds. Major Gabriel R. Paul received his promotion to brigadier general on September 5, 1862.

To Edwin Stanton, Secretary of War:

November 10, 1864.

> *This lady would be appointed Chaplain of the First Wisconsin Heavy Artillery, only that she is a woman. The President has not legally anything to do with such a question, but has no objection to her appointment.*
>
> A. *Lincoln*

Although Ella Gibson was unanimously elected chaplain of the regiment and the commanding colonel approved, Stanton rejected her appointment for fear of establishing a precedent. However, records appear to support her appointment as chaplain for the First Wisconsin Heavy Artillery, presumably thanks to Lincoln.

LINCOLN SIGNS HIS AUTOGRAPH

Your friend, A. Lincoln

Autographs and written personal sentiments between friends were very much a part of the Victorian scene. Lincoln's autograph and written sentiments were much sought after by collectors of his day. Following are several examples of Lincoln's "autograph."

Autograph. No date. Lincoln describes his definition of democracy:

> *As I would not be a slave, so I would not be a master. This expresses my idea of democracy. Whatever differs from this, to the extent of the difference, is no democracy.*

An unusual autograph note: Inscription in the autograph album of Miss Mary Smith. The date, of course, heralded the start of the American Civil War with South Carolina's firing on Fort Sumter in Charleston Harbor.

White House, April 19, 1861

Whoever in later times shall see this, and look at the date, will readily excuse the writer for not having indulged in sentiment, or poetry. With all kind regards for Miss Smith.

A. Lincoln

Lincoln gives his autograph to Mary Delahay, a second cousin whose mother, Louisiana Hanks, was a cousin (once removed) to Lincoln's mother, Nancy Hanks.

Dear Mary,
With pleasure I write my name in your Album—Ere long some younger man will be more happy to confer his name upon you—
Don't allow it, Mary, until fully assured that he is worthy of the happiness—Dec. 7. 1859
Your friend   *A. Lincoln*

LINCOLN ON SUFFRAGE

I barely suggest for your private consideration, whether some of the colored people may not be let in...

To the editor of the *Sangamo Journal*, Simeon Francis: Francis was an early and strong supporter of Lincoln. Relocating from Springfield to Oregon in 1859, Lincoln appointed Francis an Army paymaster in 1861.

June 13, 1836

I go for all sharing the privilege of the government who assist in bearing its burdens; consequently, I go for admitting all whites to the right of suffrage who pay taxes or bear arms, **by no means excluding females.**

To General James S. Wadsworth following his return from an inspection tour of freedmen in Mississippi in December of 1863: Lincoln states his policy of black suffrage.

Simeon Francis as an Army paymaster. *(Author's collection)*

January, 1864

You desire to know, in the event of our complete success in the field, the same being followed by a loyal and cheerful submission on the part of the South, if universal amnesty should not be accompanied with universal suffrage.

Now, since you know my private inclinations as to what terms should be granted to the South in the contingency mentioned, I will here add, that if our success should thus be realized, followed by such desired results, I cannot see, if universal amnesty is granted, how, under the circumstances, I can avoid exacting in return universal suffrage, or, at least, suffrage on the basis of intelligence and military service.

How to better the condition of the colored race has long been a study which has attracted my serious and careful attention; hence I think I am clear and decided as to what course I shall pursue in the premises, regarding it a religious duty, as the nation's guardian of these people, who have so heroically vindicated their manhood on the battle-field, where

in assisting to save the life of the Republic, they have demon-
strated in blood their right to the ballot, which is but the
humane protection of the flag they have so fearlessly defended.
The restoration of the Rebel States to the Union must rest
*upon the principal of civil and political **equality of both races***
(emphasis added); *and it must be sealed by general amnesty.*

To Michael Hahn, newly elected governor of free-state Louisiana:

Private   *Executive mansion*
Hon. Michael Hahn   *Washington,*
                                        March 13, 1864.
My dear Sir:
I congratulate you on having fixed your name in history
as the first-free-state Governor of Louisiana. Now you are
about to have a convention which, among other things, will
probably define the elective franchise. I barely suggest for
your private consideration, whether some of the colored people
may not be let in—as, for instance, the very intelligent, and
especially those who have fought gallantly in our ranks. They
would probably help, in some trying time to come, to keep the
jewel of liberty within the family of freedom. But this is only
a suggestion, not to the public, but to you alone. Yours truly,

A. Lincoln

LINCOLN'S LAST WRITING

Allow Mr. Ashmun & friend to come in at 9. A.M. to-morrow.

April 14.1865   *A. Lincoln*

This note is accompanied by the following statement in the hand of Congressman George Ashmun:

"The above is the last autograph of President Lincoln. It
was written and given to me at half past 8 P.M. April 14,
1865, just as he & Mrs. Lincoln were starting for the theatre
where he was assassinated."

SUGGESTED READINGS

Basler, Roy P., et. al. eds. *The Collected Works of Abraham Lincoln.* (Abraham Lincoln Association, Springfield, Illinois). New Brunswick, NJ: Rutgers University Press, 1953.

Blegan, Theodore C. *Lincoln's Imagery: A Study in Word Power.* Emerson G. Wulling, La Crosse: Sumac Press, 1954.

Braden, Waldo W. *Abraham Lincoln: Public Speaker.* Baton Rouge: Louisiana State University Press, 1988.

Kerner, Fred., ed. *A Treasury of Lincoln Quotations.* New York: Doubleday & Company, Inc., 1965.

Shaw, Archer H., ed. *The Lincoln Encyclopedia.* New York: The MacMillan Company, 1950.

Zall, P.M., ed. *Abe Lincoln Laughing.* Berkeley, Los Angeles: University of California Press, 1982.

Edward Steers, Jr., a native of Bethlehem, Pennsylvania, received his undergraduate and graduate training at the University of Pennsylvania where he earned a Bachelor's Degree in Biology and a Doctorate in Molecular Genetics. Now retired from the National Institutes of Health where he served as Deputy Scientific Director for the National Institute of Diabetes and Digestive and Kidney Diseases, Dr. Steers is a recognized authority on the life and death of Abraham Lincoln. Among his works are: *The Escape and Capture of John Wilkes Booth,* and *Lincoln: A Pictorial Biography* both published by Thomas Publications. Dr. Steers' latest work, *His Name Is Still Mudd,* will be published in 1996.

THOMAS PUBLICATIONS publishes books about the American Colonial era, the Revolutionary War, the Civil War, and other important topics. For a complete list of titles, please write to:

THOMAS PUBLICATIONS
P.O. Box 3031
Gettysburg, PA 17325